First published in Great Britain in 2007
Hansib Publications Limited
PO Box 226, Hertford SG14 3WY, England
Email: info@hansib-books.com
Website: www.hansib-books.com

ISBN 1 870518 75 6

Design and production by Graphic Resolutions, Hertfordshire, England

Printed and bound by Butler & Tanner, Somerset, England
Established in 1850, Butler and Tanner is the UK's leading book and brochure printer, with multiple
awards for exceptional quality. They are one of the greenest printing outfits in the world.

Previous page: Children at the annual Crop Over festival (Photo/Willie Alleyne)
Inside front cover: The Chalky Mount, Saint Andrew (Photo/Bruce Hemming)
Inside back cover: Bottom Bay, Saint Philip (Photo/Barbados Tourism Authority)

BARBADOS

experience the authentic Caribbean

HANSIB

mangobay

Many believe there is no better gift than the gift of a book.

In a constantly changing world, books are timeless – they capture and freeze specific moments in time. In this age of computer screens and page-less information, it is an almost outdated comfort to sit with a good book and revel in what lies between its covers.

That is why I have chosen this book about our island, our home, Barbados. Not only does it chronicle life here at this point in time, but also captures unchanging aspects that define the island and what makes it unique in the Caribbean.

I hope it will give you pleasure, as it has given me, and will encourage you to write new chapters in your own life story whenever you recall your happy memories of visiting us.

I hope it will also create an appetite for you to return to our island, and to Mango Bay, for many years to come.

Warm personal regards,

Peter J. Odle
Chairman, Mango Bay Group

Contents

Bruce Hemming

right (and cover) from top / the Barbados Jazz Festival; a chattel house; Bridgetown Port; racing at the Garrison Savannah, Saint Michael; the Lone Star Restaurant, Saint James; Heroe's Square, Bridgetown; Six Men's Bay, Saint Peter; Morgan Lewis Mill, Saint Andrew; children at the Crop Over festival; Sandy Lane beach, Saint James

left (and main cover image) / the iconic beach at Bathsheba, on the Atlantic coastline of Saint Joseph

opposite / Sunbury Plantation House, Saint Philip

ACKNOWLEDGEMENTS

Much appreciation and thank you to the following for their help and support towards the publication of *Barbados - experience the authentic Caribbean*.

Noel Lynch, Minister of Tourism; Stuart Lane, President and Chief Executive Officer, Barbados Tourism Authority; Andrew Cox, Permanent Secretary, Ministry of Tourism and Cicely Walcott, Senior Vice President, Barbados Tourism Authority.

Our team in the UK: **Managing Editor Shareef Ali**; Project Coordinator Isha Persaud; Ella Barnes, Richard Painter, Alan Cross, sub-editor Adam Licudi, design & production by Graphic Resolutions and our printers Butler and Tanner.

In Barbados our sales representative Skyviews Caribbean Limited – Managing Director Jessica Bensley and her team Verity Dawson, Maureen Stewart-Bayley, Sarah Amlot, Nicky Dover, Kerry-Ann Patrick and other members of staff. Marcia Manning for her continuing support to Hansib; Trevor Marshall for coordinating the writers in Barbados. Beverley Headley, Kim Thorpe, Sueann Tannis, Bernard Phillips and staff at Barbados Tourism Authority.

To the writers Sean Carrington, Verity Dawson, Morris Greenidge, Andrel Griffiths, Lisa Hutchinson, Susan Mahon, Marcia Manning, Trevor Marshall, Arti Meyers, Hilford Murrell, Martin Ramsay, Keith Sandiford, Ronnie McD Squires, Sueann Tannis, Andi Thornhill, Kim Thorpe, Sarah Venable, Peter Wickham and Marlon Yarde.

To the photographers Willie Alleyne and Bruce Hemming, with additional photographs from the Barbados Tourism Authority, the Barbados Government Information Service and Mount Gay Rum.

To the management and staff at Savannah Hotel, BWIA staff in London and Barbados, LIAT staff in Barbados.

To the organisations and businesses who supported the project with advance orders.

To Vicki Alton, Adrian Jones and staff at Royal Bank of Canada, Sunset Crest, St James, Emerson Clarke, Lisa Haynes, Willie Alleyne Associates and staff, Jo-anne Swyer, Lisa St John, Salena West, Chandani Persaud and Fidel Persaud. And finally, to Pamela Mary for caring so much.

Arif Ali
Bridgetown
October 2006

HANSIB PUBLICATIONS IS GRATEFUL FOR THE SUPPORT GIVEN BY
THE FOLLOWING BUSINESSES AND ORGANISATIONS:

Abacus Builders Inc.
Advanced Business Systems (ABS) Inc.
Alleyne Real Estate (A Division of Jennifer Alleyne Ltd.)
Ansa McAl (Barbados) Ltd.
Apes Hill Club
Arawak Cement Company Limited
Armstrong Agencies Ltd.
Atlantis Sea Food Inc
Atlantis Submarines Barbados Inc.
Automotive Art
Barbados Beach Club (All Inclusive Resort)
Barbados Coalition of Service Industries
Barbados Defence Force
Barbados Golf Club
Barbados Horticultural Society
Barbados Institute of Management & Productivity
Barbados International Business Promotion Corporation
Barbados Packaging Industries Ltd.
Barbados Public Workers' Co-operative Credit Union Ltd
Barbados Shipping & Trading Co. Ltd.
Barbados Tourism Authority
Barbados Tourism Investment Inc.
BHL – Banks Holdings Limited
BICO Ltd.
Bridgetown Cruise Terminals Inc.
British American Insurance Co.
Brooks Latouche Photography Ltd
Bubba's Sports Bar & Restaurant
Cable & Wireless (Barbados) Limited
Carib Rehab Ltd.
Caribbean Lifestyles Ltd.
Chickmont Foods
Cloister Bookstore Ltd
Cobblers Cove Hotel
Cole's Printery Ltd.
Collins Limited
Consolidated Finance Co. Limited
Co-operators General Insurance Co. Ltd
Daphne's Restaurant
Divi South Winds Hotel & Beach Club
Earthworks (is no ordinary) Pottery
Elegant Hotels Group
Eric Hassell & Son Ltd.
Flower Forest of Barbados Ltd.
G4S Security Services (Barbados) Ltd.
Gillespie & Steel Associates Ltd.
Goddard Enterprises Limited
Graeme Hall Nature Sanctuary
IBM World Trade Corporation

Illuminat (Barbados) Limited
Innotech Services Ltd.
InterAmericana Trading Corporation
Intimate Hotels of Barbados
Island Gold Realty & Fairways Real Estate
Island Heritage Insurance Co. Ltd.
JE Security Systems & Services Inc.
Josefs Restaurants
KPMG
Laparkan B'dos Ltd
LASCO (Barbados) Limited
Ministry of Foreign Affairs
Moore Paragon
Mount Gay Distilleries Ltd.
National Cultural Foundation Barbados
Needham's Point Holdings Ltd. with Hilton as Manager
Ocean Fisheries Ltd.
Ocean One
Ocean Park
Pages Book Stores
Palm Beach Hotel Group
Pauls Enterprises Ltd.
Pisces Restaurant
RBC Royal Bank of Canada
RBTT Bank Barbados Ltd.
Realtors Ltd.
Reefers & Wreckers
Rose and Laflamme (Barbados) Ltd
Royal Westmoreland
St. Nicholas Abbey
Sagicor Life Inc.
Scotiabank
Sea Breeze Beach Hotel
Skyviews Caribbean Ltd
South Beach Resort
Stansfeld Scott & Co. Ltd.
Sunbury Great House
Sunpower (1999) Ltd.
The Codrington School
The Lakes Development Co. Ltd.
The Restaurant at Southsea
The Sol Group
Tower Bucknall Austin
Treasure Beach Hotel
Tropical Shipping
WAMCO Data Management
Weddings...beyond Your Imagination!!
Williams Industries Inc.
Wow Group Ltd. T/A Lone Star Restaurant & Hotel

Map of Barbados,

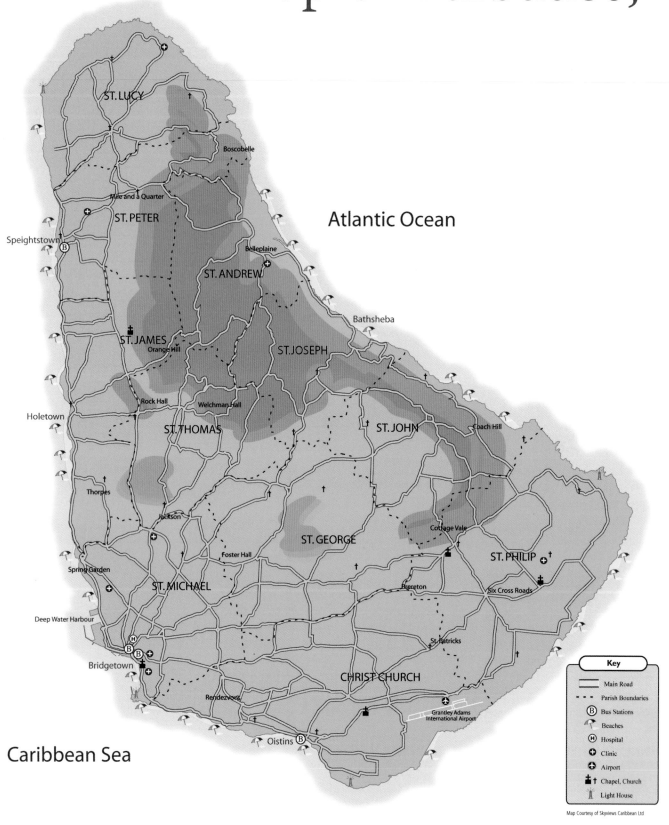

Atlantic Ocean

Caribbean Sea

Key

——	Main Road
- - -	Parish Boundaries
Ⓑ	Bus Stations
☂	Beaches
Ⓗ	Hospital
✛	Clinic
✈	Airport
⛪ †	Chapel, Church
🗼	Light House

Map Courtesy of Skyviews Caribbean Ltd

ST.LUCY

Boscobelle

Mile and a Quarter

ST.PETER

Speightstown

Belleplaine

ST.ANDREW

Bathsheba

ST.JAMES

Orange Hill

ST.JOSEPH

Rock Hall

Welchman Hall

Holetown

ST.THOMAS

ST.JOHN

Coach Hill

Thorpes

Jackson

Cottage Vale

ST.GEORGE

ST.PHILIP

Foster Hall

Spring Garden

ST.MICHAEL

Brereton

Six Cross Roads

Deep Water Harbour

St.Patricks

Bridgetown

CHRIST CHURCH

Rendezvous

Grantley Adams
International Airport

Oistins

the Flag,

The National Flag of Barbados is composed of three equal vertical panels - the outer panels of ultramarine and the centre panel of gold. A broken trident in black is in the centre of the flag. The flag is designed in the proportion 3:2. The description of the flag - Blue for the sea and sky of Barbados; Gold for the sand of its beaches. The symbol in the centre panel is the Trident of the mythical sea god, Neptune. The shaft of the Trident is broken indicating Barbados' break with its historical and constitutional ties as a former colony.

Coat of Arms

The Golden Shield of the Arms carries two Pride of Barbados flowers (the National Flower) and the Bearded Fig Tree. On either side of the shield are the supporters - on the right (dexter) is a dolphin symbolic of the fishing industry and on the left (sinister) is a pelican – named after an island which existed off Barbados but was incorporated into the Deep Water Harbour development.

Above the shield is a helmet and mantling and on a wreath is the arm and hand of a Barbadian holding two crossed pieces of sugar cane symbolic of the sugar industry. This is a saltire cross, the cross upon which Saint Andrew was crucified. Independence Day in Barbados is celebrated on 30 November, Saint Andrews Day. The Coat of Arms carries the motto "Pride and Industry".

and Anthem

In plenty and in time of need
When this fair land was young
Our brave forefathers sowed the seed
From which our pride is sprung,
A pride that makes no wanton boast
Of what is has withstood
That binds our hearts from coast to coast
The pride of nationhood

The Lord has been the people's guide
For past three hundred years
With him still on the people's side
We have no doubts or fears
Upward and onward we shall go
Inspired, exulting, free
And greater will our nation grow
In strength and unity

Chorus:
We loyal sons and daughters all
Do hereby make it known
These fields and hills beyond recall
Are now our very own.
We write our names on history's page
With expectations great
Strict guardians of our heritage
Firm craftsmen of our fate

Welcome

from the Prime Minister of Barbados, The Rt Hon Owen S Arthur

IT IS my distinct pleasure to welcome this edition of *Barbados – experience the authentic Caribbean*. In these pages you will be escorted on an unforgettable journey in an island that offers the best of what is truly Caribbean.

This book is comprehensive in scope, yet captures the essence of Barbados. It would be of interest to the potential tourist, the prudent investor, the curious reader or indeed the student or academic searching for relevant information on a unique island.

Barbados has much of what a citizen would wish to have in a relatively small package of 166-square miles. An island of quintessential natural beauty blessed with a climate of perpetual summer, the country has become one of the leading developing nations in the world.

It is fitting that this book is being produced at a time when Barbados celebrates its 40th year of Independence, for if we think in terms of the adage that 'life begins at 40', surely Barbados, which is now ranked 31st in the world by the World Economic Forum in terms of economic competitiveness, has entered the portals of the 21st century poised to join the family of developed nations.

Our country is one where there is a strong democratic impulse deeply imbedded in the national consciousness. This tradition has led to the blossoming of a democratic ethos, which has found expression in a politically stable climate that has led one Caribbean Prime Minister to describe Barbados as the best-run black society in the world.

The island is one where there is a strong commitment to nationhood, social justice, the promotion of cultural plurality and the embracing of ethnicity within the context of an evolving Caribbean integration movement. This cultural fabric has led to the development of a social integration model based on a partnership of State, labour, civil society and indeed the Church, which is so essential to nation building.

Barbados is a country that intimately realises that its greatest resource is its people and that education is inextricably linked to economic growth. The strong cultural respect for education has led Barbados to achieve a 98 per cent rate of literacy and to be the leader of the sub-region in terms of access to higher

education. The value of its human capital is reflected in the country's motto 'Pride and Industry', which is expressed in an industriousness that is part of the cultural identity of the island.

The country has laid the foundation for a diversified economy based on prudent monetary and fiscal policies, which has seen greater focus on the services sector as the main engine for economic growth.

You will find in Barbados an intricate road network, First World telecommunications system, sea and airports and a modern public transportation system.

The discerning tourist will be happy to see in Barbados beautiful white sandy beaches, bright smiling faces, captivating nightlife, the best in Caribbean and international cuisine, luxury to budget-priced accommodations, peaceful heritage sites, excellent shopping and varied sporting events.

Indeed, Barbados has now matured to the extent where the world's sporting community has reposed the confidence in the island to host the World Golf Championships Barbados World Cup in 2006 and the Final of the Cricket World Cup in 2007, the third largest sporting event on the planet.

I believe that the pictures and attendant prose are more eloquent that I am in capturing the best of Barbados in this book, and I therefore congratulate Hansib Publications on this effort, which is an excellent gift to the nation on the occasion of its 40th Anniversary Celebrations.

Rt Hon Owen S Arthur
October, 2006

"Barbados is a place where smiles are real, like the flowers of the island. It's a place where you can relax stress-free on the beach and listen to the sounds of the waves. It is an island where we cater to all people, on business or on holiday; where each one of us goes the extra mile to make sure you enjoy your visit. We're also habit-forming and welcome you year after year to our island paradise. Barbados is yours to experience and explore."

Lena Hyland, FRIENDS

Foreword

THE FIRST book Hansib produced on Barbados coincided with the 30th Anniversary of Independence in 1996.

Prime Minister Owen Arthur reminded us in his message of the adage "life begins at forty", but if you consider the progress this small country, its citizens at home and 'patriots' abroad have achieved before the 40th Anniversary one can only predict a great future for a country that we titled in our 1996 edition as *Barbados - Just Beyond Your Imagination.*

From Errol Barrow, the country's first Prime Minister to Owen Arthur the man at the helm as we go to press, the politicians, irrespective of which party was in power; have set an example of moral and integrity, which only a few countries have achieved.

With limited natural resources except for its people, sun, sand and sea, meant that the government, guided by the wishes of its citizens, came to the conclusion that stability and sensible governance was what Barbadians wanted, and so inspiring what Prime Minister Arthur Owen said in his message:

"Our country is one where there is a strong democratic impulse deeply imbedded in the national consciousness. This tradition has led to the blossoming of a democratic ethos which has found expression in a politically stable climate that has led one Caribbean Prime Minister to describe Barbados as the best run black society in the world."

The 270,000 people of Barbados understand and respect their tourism industry, the largest single employer, receiving four times as many visitors as the population, many of whom are returnees. Regular visitors cannot help but see the continuing improvement and modernisation from the air and seaports to the hotels, sporting facilities and entertainment.

A stable country attracts international investors and Barbados continues to improve on the quality of service and personnel available to potential investors.

Visitors to this country will experience the authentic Caribbean.

Arif Ali
Bridgetown
October 2006

Willie Alleyne

Barbados:– Experience authentic Caribbean

top / perhaps Barbados' most iconic beach – Bathsheba, Saint Joseph

above / fine dining at The Cliff, Saint James

opposite / a reveller at the Grand Kadooment, the highlight of the annual Crop Over festival

previous pages / Six Men's Bay, Saint Peter; Paynes Bay Beach, Saint James; Farley Hill Recreational Park, Saint Peter

Photos: Bruce Hemming

Barbados. The spot in the Caribbean where the sun rises first. Barbados. Land of the silver flying fish. Barbados. Follow on to an authentic Caribbean experience. Barbados.

THE **Arawak Indians** inhabited the island for over 2000 years. **Caribs** then occupied the island, but while relics of their sojourn in Barbados have been found, the actual manner of their departure is clouded in mystery. By the time that the **Portuguese** arrived in **1536**, the Carib population had vanished without trace. The Portuguese did not remain, but let loose wild hogs and gave the island its name.

When the **English**, on the ship the *Olive Blossom*, landed on Barbados in **1625**, they found it uninhabited. They claimed it for King James of England. Eighty settlers and 10 slaves arrived on the *William and John* on February 17, 1627. The area in which they landed is now called **Holetown**. The settlement would develop rapidly into England's wealthiest colony.

From **Independence Day**, November 30, 1966 until now, Barbados moved on a determined path to be the most developed island in the Caribbean and one of the most admired small island states in the world. The island of 166 square miles has been consistently among the leading developing countries in the

above / history preserved at Farley Hill National Park, Saint Peter

top / Harrison's Cave, Saint Thomas

middle / a child observes a ray at Ocean Park, Christ Church

world, according to the United Nations' Human Development Index. The nation's sons and daughters, now numbering **270,000**, have in its history chalked up a number of exceptional distinctions.

Along with the people, two other great assets to the tourism industry have been **Grantley Adams International Airport**, 11 miles from the capital, **Bridgetown**, and the **Bridgetown Port**, just a mile from the centre of the city. These two major points of entry are the best of their kind in the Caribbean and are still expanding! On arrival in Barbados, a country divided into **11 parishes**, visitors notice very quickly that the diversity around the fringes is breathtaking. In the west and in the south, coconut palms sway on sandy white beaches before a calm blue sea. By contrast, in the north and east, the palms sway on off-white beaches before a cliff or large, picturesque boulders attacked by a turbulent ocean. The rolling hills of the **Scotland District** are also a welcome distraction from the flat terrain of the west and south, as the picturesque fields of lush sugar cane counteract the effect of developed towns and villages.

Accommodation on the island meets all tastes and budgets: the all-inclusive, the small hotel; the self-contained apartment; the guesthouse or the villa. All are supervised by the Quality Assurance Department of the Barbados Tourism Authority. These hotels offer exquisite dining in beautiful settings, as do the private restaurants, which may specialise in the local fare or international cuisine, but serve their dishes with a unique Caribbean flavour.

Of course, 'sea, sand and sun' is offered on Barbados; but it also caters for another triple 's': sightseeing, shopping and sports. Sightseeing is certainly a treat. Bajan Helicopters offer aerial views of paradise; a visit to **Harrison's Cave** is an entry into a fantasy land below the earth; the miracle of underwater life is revealed by the **Atlantis submarine,** while the new attraction, **Ocean Park** offers the experience of walking underwater without getting wet.

Arguably the most breathtaking view in Barbados is from **Cherry Tree Hill**. Plantation houses like **Sunbury** have their own exquisite charm – with its open bedrooms, its prized carriage collection and little museum. The intriguing ruin of **Farley Hill** is also not to be missed. With a grandeur worthy of the silver screen, it features in the 1957 movie *Island in the Sun*, but was destroyed by fire not long afterwards and taken over by the Barbados Government as a recreational park. There is a view from the woody Farley Hill, rivalling that of Cherry Tree Hill.

The military history of Barbados has also left its mark. The **Barbados Museum**, a former British military prison, offers a small but very interesting curiosity collection tracing Barbados from its earliest days. There is the **Gun Hill Signal Station**, wonderfully preserved by the Barbados National Trust, and the magnificent coral stone lion carved by recuperating soldiers to represent the might of the British Empire, as well as **the Garrison Area**, rich in the relics of the nation's military past. There, one can find Bush Hill House, the only place outside of the USA where George Washington spent a night.

Andromeda Botanic Gardens, **Flower Forest** and **Orchid World** are abundant in exotic blooms. As a testimony to the beauty and quality of the flowers found in Barbados, the local Horticultural Society has won more than 10 Gold Medals at the prestigious Chelsea Flower Show in England.

A visit to the Nature Sanctuary in **Graeme Hall Swamp** provides a peaceful home for mostly migrant birds, while a visit to **the Barbados Wildlife Reserve** virtually guarantees a sighting of an African green monkey, the only plentiful wild animal on the island, though visitors may be lucky enough to view them elsewhere, even in residential areas. There is no more intriguing, mesmerizing creature on this earth.

Rum was first distilled in Barbados and the spirit gives the raison d'etre for other attractions: **Mount Gay Rum Visitors' Centre**; the **Foursquare Rum Factory and Heritage Park**; the **Malibu Visitors' Centre**. You can become hooked on the rum punch with its apparently harmless golden glow! Not to be outdone, the home of the local beer, **Banks Breweries** also offers a highly popular tour. Beverages for teetotallers: how about a coconut and straw; a nicely blended fruit punch; a mauby or ginger beer?

Heritage and eco-tourism are in vogue the world over and Barbados is no exception. An enjoyable excursion is the **Hike Barbados**, which offers free exercise and knowledge as hikers weekly undertake different trails according to their stamina.

When it comes to duty-free shopping, look no further than **Broad Street**. There you can shop for premium brands in electronic goods, clothing, glass and crystal ornaments, china, cameras, perfumes and liquor. Designer clothes can also be found in boutiques, both on the west and the south coast, while numerous local designers are sure to produce something stunningly different.

Not only in clothes can you benefit from the local touch. Pottery, basketry, paper, paintings, wirework, shellwork... all these can be found in **Pelican Village**, where 'made in Barbados' is guaranteed. Quality souvenirs are also available in the 'Best of Barbados' shops, where everything is either designed or made on the island.

above / cricketing legend Sir Garfield Sobers, enjoys a round on one of Barbados' many golf courses

top / the historic Garrison Savannah area of Saint Michael

middle / Graeme Hall Swamp, Christ Church

In Barbados, one sport is worshipped above all others – cricket. Over the years the island has produced some of the best in the sport, chief among whom is the only living National Hero, the **Right Excellent Sir Garfield Sobers**, OCC, widely acknowledged as 'the greatest cricketer the world has ever seen'. But, nowadays, the word 'golf' is on everyone's lips, even Sir Garfield's. Visitors who want to develop a swing like Tiger Woods could practise here in Barbados at the glorious Royal Westmoreland Golf and Country Club or the perennially pristine Sandy Lane Golf Club, with its prestigious Green Monkey, Country Club and Old Nine courses. They should also check out the Barbados Golf Club at Durants in Christ Church, which has an 18-hole championship course (and the full works) open to the public. Tennis, horseracing, hockey, running, football, cycling, gliding, parasailing, surfing, windsurfing, water-skiing, jet-skiing, sailing, deep-

Willie Alleyne

sea fishing (a good family day out) are just some of the other land and water sports that can be experienced in Barbados. Swimming or rather snorkelling with the turtles is the latest craze. Note the season for turtles in Barbados; for the leatherback, it is March-July, while for the hawksbill, it is April-October.

There is fun to be had on the **Jolly Roger** pirate ship or the **Harbour Master** riverboat. More exclusive enjoyment can be experienced on the smaller catamarans, while back on land the island comes to life in the evening at after-dinner shows such as the 'Bajan Roots and Rhythms' and at night clubs like **After Dark, Harbour Lights** and **The Boatyard**.

Special entertainment throughout the year is provided by the festivals like the **Barbados Jazz Festival** in January, which over the years has featured an excellent blend of local performers and international artistes like Patti LaBelle, Alicia Keyes, Lionel Richie and many more. Next is the **Holetown Festival** in February, which commemorates the first landing and settlement in Barbados. Holders Season in March is the most sophisticated festival, offering the best in opera, Shakespeare, and several surprising art forms. **Oistins Fish Festival** in April is a novel way of celebrating the livelihood of the fishing village that gives it its name (NB – You don't have to wait for Easter to experience the excitement of Oistins. Every weekend, visitors and locals meet by the fish market to view arts and crafts, listen to the latest in local music and, first and foremost, sit on benches together to sample in the open air the delightful local cuisine, including fish and macaroni cheese or cou-cou, Bajan favourites). **Gospelfest**, featuring various enjoyable ways of giving praise to the Lord, is in May, while **Crop Over**, which spreads from July to August, is the ultimate means of tasting all the best of Barbados culture.

After all the excitement, inevitably, the sun must set. At that point, those who are lucky will see the rare, almost mythical, green flash. Those who do not will still be happy. They are still in Barbados and are dreaming of buying a home here. Investing in paradise? Not a bad idea at all!

/ *Kim Thorpe*

above / flagwaving stiltmen at the Grand Kadooment – highlight of the Crop Over festival

top / US singer and songwriting star Lionel Ritchie headlining the Barbados Jazz Festival

middle / the Jolly Roger pirate ship sails the seas off Barbados – laden with tourists and other party-seekers

opposite / one of the many performers at the Jazz Festival

overleaf / cloudscape from Sandy Lane on Barbados' Saint James coast

Bruce Hemming

Bruce Hemming

A Short History

above / a bearded fig tree – which may have given Barbados its name

top / a petroglyph carved in Spinghead Cave, Saint James – the closest written record of Barbados' earliest inhabitants

opposite / the rugged terrain of the Chalky Mount, Saint Andrew – on Barbados' Atlantic northeast coast

THE island of Barbados has a singular history. Of all the Caribbean islands, it is the only one in which there were no 'Amerindians' or indigenous people living at the time of English colonisation, and its history therefore runs counter to the usual regional development of a bruising encounter between the two races of indigenous people and 'whites'. The island is one of only three (the others being Antigua and Montserrat) that were not 'discovered' by the Genoese explorer, Christopher Columbus between 1492 and 1504. It is the only island in the Caribbean that was 'discovered' by the **Portuguese**, or has a Portuguese name, and it has never been possessed or conquered by any European state except England.

That collection of facts should be enough to render Barbados a Caribbean historical phenomenon, but the list does not stop there. Barbados is not in the Caribbean Sea, but lies in the **Atlantic** approximately 100 miles south-east of St Vincent, its closest neighbour, and is therefore the nearest island to the continent of Africa, being approximately 3,500 miles west of Senegal. Barbados was therefore strategically placed to become the entrepot for the African slave trade to the New World and the first port of call for the slave ships of the non-Iberian European states when the commerce in 'Black Cargoes' or West African natives reached its zenith in the 18th century.

Another interesting historical point is that mystery and controversy still surrounds the naming of the island by Portuguese sailors, who under the captaincy of Pedro a Campos, landed on the island in 1536 as the first Europeans to set foot on it and gave it the title **'Los Barbados'**, which is loosely interpreted to mean **'The island of Bearded Fig Trees'**. This interpretation has been challenged in recent decades by a Guyanese scholar, Dr Richard Allsopp, who in the late 20th century raised

Bruce Hemming

the question of whether the title did not refer to 'Bearded Men' rather than fig trees and whether Africans were not visitors to or settlers on the island before the Europeans ever came to it.

These are all issues to occupy the historians of the future, but it is fair to say that Barbados, 'the singular island' as it was referred to in order to distinguish it from 'The Bahamas' and 'The Bermudas' in European geographical writings, has had a fascinating though relatively unspectacular history when compared with Jamaica, Cuba, Puerto Rico, Hispaniola (Haiti and the Dominican Republic) or Trinidad, the other prominent Caribbean islands. According to historian Karl Watson the first settlers on Barbados were the **Arawak**, who entered the island from the region of Guyana highlands and settled along the northern, western and southern coasts. According to archaeologists, this was approximately 1500 years before the time of Christ. After them came groups of fishing and hunting folk, who pursued a living in a peaceful way for over 1400 years. However, it is not yet established whether they were **Taino** (Arawaks) only or **Kalingo** (Caribs). Opinion among historians and archaeologists is that both culture groups existed on the island, which they called *Ichirouganaim* – 'big red island with sharp white teeth' – and scholars are united in the belief that the Taino left the island to escape the marauding Kalingo, preferring to live in peace in another island than to die at the hands of these invaders.

However, as far as we are able to gather from archaeological evidence, the Kalingo left *Ichirouganaim* about 50 years before Columbus made his first landing in the region at Hispaniola some 800 miles to the west. Barbados had been uninhabited therefore for nearly a hundred years when an English ship landed in 1625, having been blown off-course while sailing from the Guianas. The ship, the *Olive Blossom,* landed at an inlet which reminded them so much of a part of the River Thames, which runs through London, that the captain, Henry Powell, named it 'The Hole', later to become **Holetown**. His sailors made a brief landing and claimed the island in the name of 'James, King of England'.

In late 1626 a ship, the *William and John,* left England with 20 crew members and 60 intending settlers and sailed for Barbados on a colonising voyage. Along the way they captured a Spanish galleon and took on board between six and 12 African slaves, brought them to the island and so inaugurated both the settlement of Barbados and the slave trade to the island (A recent study, however, by local historian Morris Greenidge, in his book *Holetown: Settlement Revisited,* has challenged some of these factual details).

Powell had instructions from his employer, William Courteen, to establish a strong English colony as quickly as possible and to utilise the skills of the indigenous Guianese Amerindians with whom the English were acquainted. Under an agreement Powell made with the Dutch Guiana Governor, the Amerindians were brought to the island to help the colonists plant and manure the crops and launch the colony on a path of sustained economic development. It would appear that this arrangement worked to the mutual satisfaction of the three parties and some 30 Amerindians came to Barbados bringing with them

cassava, sweet potato, tobacco, pineapples and other fruits for planting. Regrettably, the agreement broke down and the Amerindians, who had come to Barbados of their own free will, were enslaved and separated from wives, parents and children. Forced labour now became the means by which Barbados was cultivated in **tobacco** and it became the norm over the next two centuries as Barbados became transformed from a subsistence economy with a moderate export sector, to one which was based on the plantation system and driven by the export of **cane sugar**.

By 1628 Barbados began to take shape as an English colony. Its fledgling port **Bridgetown** (Indian Bridge town) superseded Holetown as the capital, and the Anglican Church was established as the Church of English citizens. The Africans were, of course, omitted from Christian congregations. The English settlers, their African slaves and the Amerindians 'contract labourers' from Dutch Guiana set about the arduous task of clearing the forest in order to plant their first crops of vegetables, corn and root crops for subsistence and tobacco for export. By 1631, over 50 per cent of the land had been **deforested**.

The political situation became complicated as two rival factions of Englishmen, the **Courteens** and the **Earl of Carlisle,** literally fought over who should take Barbados into the 'brave new world' that beckoned it. In the end Carlisle triumphed, partly because he held a proprietary grant for the Lesser Antilles, granted by King Charles I of England in 1628. For the next 32 years Barbados was a proprietary colony ruled by the appointees of the Earl of Carlisle, who acknowledged the English monarch as his overlord.

This was perhaps the most revolutionary time period in the history of Barbados until another 32-year era, 1937 to 1969. In the period from 1628 to 1660 a number of economic, political and social developments occurred, propelling Barbados from a tiny colonial backwater into the forefront of the English socio-economic revolution that saw the Slave Trade produce an era of unparalleled wealth within the British Isles.

During this period the island's institutions received their final shape. In addition to the Anglican Church, limited democracy made its appearance with the creation of a **House of Assembly** with two elected representatives from each of the 11 parishes. Voting was restricted (until 1843) to free, white, property-owning Christian males. Legislation originated from this body, as did money bills. These were then passed on to the Legislative council, made up of 12 senior nominated individuals chosen from among the island's richest planters. The Governor, in turn, vetted the legislation and passed it on to England for Royal Assent. This was the famous '**Parliamentary Democracy**' that was established in 1639 by **Governor Henry Hawley** and which gave Barbados considerable autonomy in relation to the imperial government.

Another institution that was founded in this era was the Vestry or Local Government system that was anchored in the **11 parishes**, all of which had been delineated by 1645 and which were chaired by the Parish Rectors. The

above / the deforestation of Barbados – over half of which was done by 1631 – was achieved mainly through burning

opposite top / Ligon's Map of Barbados made by John Swan in around 1640. It clearly shows camels as beasts of burden, an experiment that did not stand the test of time

opposite bottom / an early 20th century photograph of sugar cane being harvested – a scene perhaps not much changed for over 300 years

above / a traditional chattel house

top / copper pot stills at the Mount Gay Rum Distillery. Stills like these have been used since the 1700s

Vestry, made up of the property holders of the parish, were empowered to collect parish taxes and rents and to spend such monies on parish roads, poor relief, education, emergency relief and security.

Yet another institution that emerged in this early period was the militia, comprising free (white) males, aged between 16 and 60, who were required to enrol for the defence of their colony. The militia provided both internal security and a measure of protection against invasion.

By far the most spectacular development of the island in the period 1630 to 1660 was economic. In 1640, following experiments conducted by a Dutch Jew, Pieter Brewer, who was specially recruited from Bahia in Brazil to assess the prospects of sugar cane cultivation on a large scale, the island began to shift to **sugar cane**. Tobacco, the island's earliest export crop, had failed by 1637 owing to a glut on the English market. The production of sugar and its by-products, rum and molasses, would become the island's principal activity for the next 320 years (until 1960) and bring about changes so profound and lasting that it would be termed the **'Sugar Revolution'**.

Everything else that occurred paled in comparison, even the 1651 invasion of the island by **Sir George Ayescue** to subdue the Royalists, who continued stubbornly to support the Royalist cause after the execution of Charles I in 1649. Between 1640 and 1670 the dense rain forests of Barbados were systematically cut down to provide land for the Sugar Revolution. This backbreaking work was carried out by English, Welsh, Irish and Scottish young men. These 'Indentured Servants,' some volunteers, some victims of the **English Civil War**, came as bondsmen or contract labourers serving for at least five years during which they cut down the forest, planted sugar cane, harvested the crops and hoped to receive plots of land in return. This did not satisfy the demand for unlimited supplies of labour and by the end of the 1640s, large numbers of African captives were being brought into the island to serve as gang slaves on the sugar plantations. The system of **'chattel'** slavery entrapped the blacks for life, but the white indentured servants, later to be called 'Poor Whites', 'Red Legs' or 'Eckie-Beckies', experienced a form of semi-slavery or cruel bond-service for periods of 5-10 years before they could be released. One such unfortunate indentured servant was the famous buccaneer, **Sir Henry Morgan**. After a time, several of these indentured whites became militia tenants.

By 1720 the system of indentured white bond-service was ended, but slavery of the blacks from West Africa continued until 1838. The Barbados slave system became the model on which every other British Caribbean colony was patterned. It featured severe slave laws, gang labour for blacks over a 12-hour working day and barbarous punishments for infractions of the slave laws. Despite being what Karl Watson call "the civilised island", Barbados was a Caribbean colony in which the planter class consolidated its political and socio-economic control to the maximum. Several laws were passed, notably those against slaves carrying weapons, meeting in large groups or buying and selling agricultural produce. The planter class succeeded so well that, after the minor revolts of 1649, 1675 and 1694, there were no more uprisings for 122 years until the '**Bussa Rebellion**' of 1816 shattered the complacency of the white planter community.

Barbados became an extremely prosperous and heavily populated island before the end of its first century of recorded history. By 1690 the population was 70,000 and visitors described it as '**the most valuable piece of real estate**' in the western world. By 1750 the population was approximately 100,000 of which 65,000 were slaves, 18,000 were white and 1500 were bi-racial 'mulattoes,' some of them being 'Free Coloureds'. The population also contained the remnants of the tiny Jewish population that had been extremely influential in the early development of the island and some Portuguese from Madeira and the Guianas.

By this time Barbados was easily one of Britain's most prosperous islands in the region with 508 sugar estates producing high tonnages of **Muscovado sugar** on 100,000 of the 106,000 acres. This prosperity lasted for another 30 years when the American Revolution disrupted trade between North America and Britain's Caribbean colonies. Along with other colonies, Barbados suffered loss of precious food imports and it was one of those territories in which, to stave off famine among the slaves, the breadfruit was introduced after 1789.

In addition, the first of three most powerful **hurricanes**, that of 1780 (the two others were in 1898 and 1955) killed 4,326 people and destroyed much of the sugar cane crop. However, the island survived these environmental and economic crises better than other islands. Over the next 150 years, the island would encounter and overcome similar crises, largely because of its strongly entrenched traditional agricultural practices, the quality of its sugar, molasses and rum products and the unlimited supplies of cheap black labour. This marked out Barbados from the other colonies and ensured the economic stability of the island.

The 19th century saw Barbados face the most significant event in its history thus far, the **Abolition of Slavery**, in 1838. It was preceded by the Abolition of the Slave Trade in 1807 and the Bussa uprising of 1816. The island's authorities fought bitterly against the Emancipation Act of 1833, which liberated their 82,807 black and brown slaves because they were wedded to the system of slavery and forecast the ruin of the sugar industry after Emancipation.

However, ruin did not occur. Using the legal weapon of the Masters and Servants Act, which they put into place in 1840, the plantocracy instituted a system of neo-slavery or economic serfdom over the next 100 years, effectively coercing black ex-slaves and their descendants into remaining on the sugar plantations as cowed landless labourers. Prosperity was therefore secured, "on the backs of black" as Hilary Beckles' phrase indicates. The Masters and Servants Act, the Located Labourers system and the Vagrancy Act were all designed to restrict the freedom of movement and choice of job of the ex-slaves, and they worked effectively. Even though wages were higher in neighbouring territories, namely Trinidad and British Guiana, emigration was discouraged as planters wanted to secure labour force at low wages. Later in the 19th century, Trinidad and Guianese

above / the statue of Lord Nelson, Heroes' Square, Bridgetown. Erected in 1813 – almost thirty years before its larger namesake in London. Nelson was hailed by Barbadians as a deliver from a possible French invasion of 1805. Later that year he was to die at the Battle of Trafalgar.

top / the Bussa Statue on the ABC Highway – honouring the uprising of 1816, which took place over two decades before the abolition of slavery

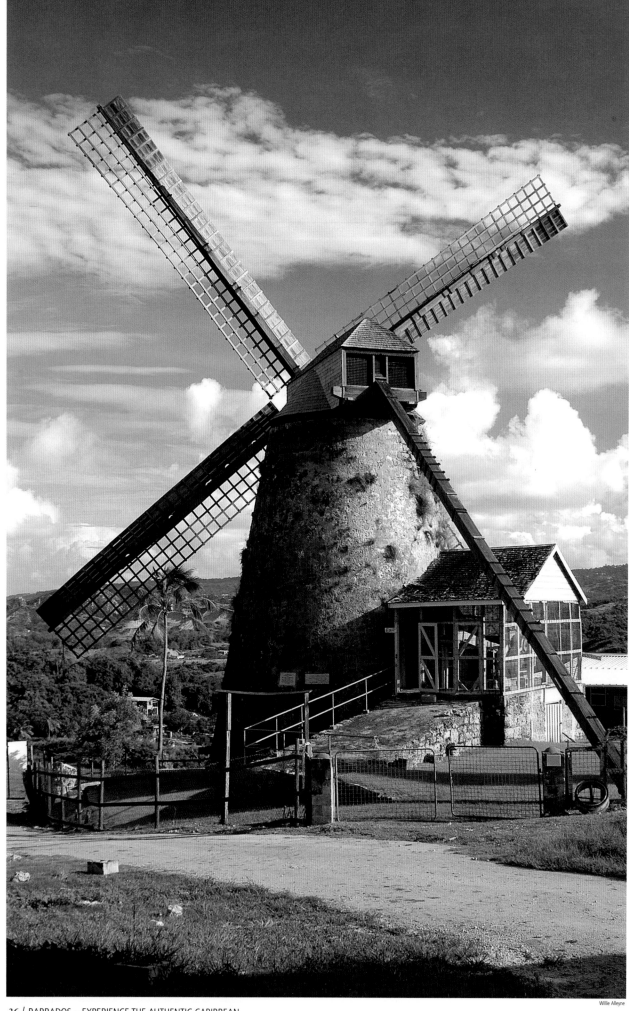

Willie Alleyne

planters recruited hundreds of Barbadian labours in a systematic programme that ended in the 1920s in British Guiana and in the 1940s in Trinidad.

Despite this loss of labourers, and the Cholera epidemic of 1854, the island continued its relentless path towards material prosperity. The white population remained relatively large, being 13,000 at Emancipation, 16,500 in 1870, 15,000 in 1900 and 14,000 in 1937. The Black population was 105,904 in 1871, 121,000 in 1900 and 135,000 in 1937. This demographic constancy enabled the plantation system to survive until the 1990s and kept Blacks anchored at the bottom of the society until the 1960s. The building of the **Panama Canal** between 1904 and 1915 helped to relieve some of the population pressure as 20,000 black Barbadians journeyed to the isthmus to work as 'Silver Men', (lesser-paid workers) on the 'Big Ditch'.

Over the 100 years following 1838, some outstanding individuals emerged to narrow the boundaries between white and black. **Samuel Jackman Prescod**, **Sarah Ann Gill**, **London Bourne** and **W Conrad Reeves**, each in their own way, helped to win small victories and concessions for the blacks at the bottom of the society in the first 60 years after Emancipation. In the next 40 years, **Charles Duncan O'Neal**, **Clennel Wickham**, **Clement Payne** and **Grantley Adams** led the fight against white control of the socio-economic and political institutions in the island. By 1937 Barbados was ripe for social conflagration and it came in the form of urban disturbances against the chronic ills of low wages, under-housing, and racial bullying on the plantations. The rhetoric of Clement Payne stirred up the masses who took the law into their own hands when he was deported to his native Trinidad.

Over a three-day period in 1937 (July 26-28), the Barbadian masses rioted for the first time since the **Confederation Riots** of 1876. These disturbances, which sent shock waves through the white elite and middle-classes, were the most serious in the island's history and helped alert the British Colonial Office to the fact that "a study of the British Caribbean is a Study of Poverty" as W M McMillan had written in 1929.

This was the turning point in the history of Barbados and over the next 70 years, the society became so transformed as to be unrecognisable by the first decade of the 21st century. There was a '**quiet revolution**' in politics, by which Grantley Adams and his Barbados Labour Party ultimately broke the power of the white oligarchs in Parliament. **Errol W Barrow**, who completed Adams' rout of the white politicians so that by 1966 when Independence came to Barbados there were only four white members of the elected House of Assembly, carried through this 'revolution'. By 1989 there were none, a stark contrast to 1936 when 20 of the 24 members of the elective Chamber were white. This group's involvement in the political process has been limited since 1966 to representation in the Senate or Upper House of appointed legislators.

Full **democracy** came to Barbados in 1951 and two mass-based political parties, the **Democratic Labour Party** (DLP), founded in 1955 and the oldest political

above / the statue of Sir Grantley Adams outside Government Headquarters in Bridgetown. Adams, the 'Father of Democracy', was Barbados' first Premier and the first Prime Minister of the West Indies Federation

top / a pro-independence march on the way to a political meeting in Bridgetown, 1965

opposite / the Morgan Lewis Mill, Saint Andrew, ceased operation in 1947. It is now a monument to the era when sugar was 'king'

overleaf / Heroes' Square and the Parliament Buildings, Bridgetown

Willie Alleyne

party in the Commonwealth Caribbean, the **Barbados Labour Party** (BLP), founded in April 1938, have alternated in power since 1951.

In that epoch-making year, the BLP 'won the government' and ruled for 10 years under Adams (knighted in 1954) and **H G Cummins**, his successor, when Adams became Prime Minister of the West Indies Federation of 1958-1962. Errol Barrow's DLP won in 1961 and took Barbados to Independence in 1966. By 1976 the BLP under **J M G M 'Tom' Adams** was back in power, ruling until 1986.

The death of Sir Grantley Adams in 1970 took away the island's 'Father of Democracy', while the death of his son, Tom in 1985 and Barrow himself in 1987, marked the end of an era of robust political decolonisation. Over the next seven years, two less charismatic political leaders **Erskine (Sir Lloyd) Sandiford** and **H Bernard (Sir Harold) St John**, alternated as Prime Ministers in a period of end-of-century transition. In 1994 the wheel turned dramatically back to the Barbados Labour Party, led by a young University of the West Indies-educated economist, **Owen S Arthur**, who combined the astuteness of Sir Grantley, the courage of Errol Barrow and the visionary genius of Tom Adams. To these skills he has added his own unique populist orientation, which has kept him fully in touch with the people at large and has been the decisive factor in his party holding the reins of power for 12 years and three terms of office. The party has presided over Barbados' continued prosperity and has kept the island firmly on course to be a '**developed nation**' by 2015. When one considers the fact that Barbados has kept its envied position as a 'middle-class nation' for over 300 years, mainly on the basis of sugar-cane agriculture, such a possibility is not out of the question.

The story of Barbados' historical development has been told mainly in terms of political and economic activity, but the island has also been a theatre of much growth and development in other areas of national life since the abolition of slavery in 1838. In education, the island has been a regional leader in primary, secondary and tertiary institutions of all ages, with **Codrington College** a theological seminary leading the way, followed by **Harrison College**, **Lodge School**, **Queen's College** and **Combermere School**. The island received its first full **University** campus in 1964 but the society has been remarkable for its dedication to education for all of its population for over 150 years and for helping to educate the rest of the region.

In economic terms, the island went through its second 'revolution,' the **tourism revolution** of 1958 to the present day, a consequence of which is that Barbados has re-branded itself in 50 years as a major tourism destination, catering to the average traveller as well as the 'high-end' visitors. This is perhaps its most remarkable achievement and has catapulted Barbados to the forefront of economic growth and development in the region. The benefits of tourism are obvious and extensive and Barbadians now enjoy a lifestyle and living standard above that of most other regional countries. Improvements have come in sea and airport development so that the island now possesses First-World facilities in areas of land sports, heritage sites, conference buildings and ground transportation.

top / Codrington College – leading the way in establishing Barbados' reputation in the field of education

above & opposite / the tourism revolution – windsurfing and snorkelling off Barbados' idyllic west coast

Willie Alleyne

The island has been a model of economic prudence since 1966 and has the enviable status of being the only Commonwealth Caribbean country to keep its currency at the same level since Independence. Indeed, Barbados has made such a success of sovereignty that economic analysts now speak of a 'Barbados model' of economic growth and development, replacing the 'Puerto Rican' model of the mid-20th century, as the ideal path to economic development and national industrialisation by small countries with open export-driven economies. Today, Barbados faces the future with the assurance that although its traditional economic 'mainstay' – sugar – is dying, the society is striding onwards to a future built more on services and the stimulation of non-sugar agriculture, as well as tourism and the off-shore sector. In the 1930s, Barbados was a theatre of hunger, sickness, poverty and low life expectancy among its largest black population despite the ostentatious wealth of its white elite.

By 2006, Barbados had been transformed economically and in every other area of life. Its population has a higher life expectancy than every other Caribbean nation except Cuba and its list of centenarians is larger, per capita, than any other country except Japan.

On the social field, Barbados has been host to a growing Indian community since 1910 and this has enriched the island's culture. More recently, smaller groupings of other races have migrated to the island from other parts of the world and also from around the region, giving Barbados a multi-ethnic, multi-racial profile in the 21st century.

Finally, the island has discovered its true cultural self. Once thought of as an island of "English Rustics in Black Skins", according to Sidney Greenfield, since Independence Barbados has realised its true value as a typical Caribbean country with a strong substratum of African music and theatrical heritage. **Crop Over** a slave ceremony of celebration now heralds the fact that the cultural profile of Barbados is one of the highest and brightest in the region. The island now boasts seven major annual festivals and its literacy level is above 90 per cent. The country is thus a textbook example of 'small is beautiful, bountiful and productive'. It is a zone of peace in a Caribbean that can sometimes be turbulent; its ethnic groups live in peaceful co-existence.

/ Trevor Marshall

above / a man dressed as a green monkey attracts the attentions of a reveller during the Crop Over parade

top & opposite / the culmination of the annual Crop Over festival – the Grand Kadooment

middle / soaking-up the atmosphere at the Barbados Jazz Festival

overleaf / Barbados in bloom – a flamboyant tree in Holetown, Saint James

Bruce Hemming

Notable Dates in the History of Barbados

1000-500 BC / First stone age Arawak settlers arrived.

100 AD / Second culture group arrived from South America.

500-600 / Third settlement by Troumassoid people.

1300 / Fourth culture group, the Suazoids arrived.

1500-20 / Carib occupation mysteriously ends.

1625 / An English ship returning from a trading voyage to Brazil touched at Barbados and took possession in the name of James I of England.

1627 / Founding of the Colony – Government comprised the Governor appointed by the island's 'Owners' (The Lord Proprietor) and a Council appointed in turn by the Governor.

1629 / The island was divided into six parishes.

1637 / One account states that sugar cane was first introduced to this island in this year.

1639 / Birth of Parliament. Representatives chosen from among the resident freeholders to sit with the original Council as a Legislative body.

1640 / Most writers agree that the manufacture of sugar started in the early 1640s.

1645 / The island was divided into eleven parishes. The Assembly comprised 22 elected members – two from each parish.

1651 / On February 16, the inhabitants of the island declared their independence of the Commonwealth of England

1652 / Articles of Agreement signed, January 11, between England and Barbados ensuring the 'Rights of the People'. Ratified in English Parliament on August 18.

1663 / A Postal Agency was established on the island to handle overseas mail.

1698 / The Act to declare and ascertain the rights and powers of the General Assembly of the island was proclaimed.

1731 / The first Barbados newspaper, the *Barbados Gazette*, was published by David Harry and Samuel Keimer.

1745 / Barbados had the first institution of higher learning to be established in a British colony when Codrington College, an affiliate of the University of Durham in England, was opened in St John.

1766 / Bridgetown was destroyed by fire.

1807 / Abolition of the Slave Trade.

1816 / A slave uprising led by the slave Bussa and a free mulatto, Washington Franklin.

1817 / The free coloured were first allowed to give evidence in court.

1826 / Legislation to ameliorate the condition of slaves was passed.
The first verdict to establish the right of a slave to protection under the common law was given when Chief Justice John Renn Hampden sentenced John Archer, a white man to a year's imprisonment for manslaughter.

1831 / Free coloured men were given the vote.

1834 / Slavery was abolished and an enforced four-year apprenticeship period was established.

1835 / The Royal Barbados Police Force was established.

1838 / August 1, emancipation of the slaves.

1840 / Legislation enacted to allow coloured men to sit in the House of Assembly.

1843 / Bridgetown became a separate constituency with two elected members. First coloured representative (Samuel Jackman Prescod) elected to the Assembly.

1847 / The founding of the Public Library.

1850 / The first Education Act was passed.

1851 / The inland mail service was authorised.

1852 / The first Barbados postage stamps were issued.

1861 / Waterworks established in Bridgetown.

1876 / Confederation riots.

1878 / Elementary education was introduced.

1881 / The Executive Committee Act passed – the first step towards representative Government – a direct result of the 'Confederation Riots'.

1884 / Franchise fixed at 50 pounds property requirement.

1885 / Barbados separated from Government of the Windward Islands.

1886 / Piped water extended to rural districts.

1889 / Establishment of the Royal Barbados Police Force Band.

1891 / Executive Committee (Consolidation) Act passed.

1924 / Charles Duncan O'Neal founded the Democratic League, the island's first organised black political group.

1934 / The election of Grantley Adams to the House of Assembly gave the black population their first real spokesman in the legislature since Prescod in 1843.

1937 / 'The Disturbances' – The 1937 Riots occurred.

1938 / This year saw the birth of the Barbados Labour Party.

1940 / The Trade Union Act, which was passed in 1939, came into force on August 1, 1940.
The General Election saw for the first time in the history of the country a political party with a clearly defined programme, offer a slate of candidates to be elected to the House of Assembly.

1941 / The Barbados Workers' Union was registered on October 4.

1944 / Franchise lowered from 50 pounds to 20 pounds for property requirements – women allowed to vote.

1946 / The 'Bushe Experiment' – the birth of party politics; the majority leader in the House to elect the House members to sit in Executive Committee and also to be leader of the House and Head of Government.

1950 / Full representative government was established when Universal Adult Suffrage was introduced. At the same time the maximum life of the House was extended from three to five years.

1954 / Ministerial Government was established.

1955 / The Democratic Labour Party was formed by a group that broke away from the Barbados Labour Party.

1958 / Barbados became part of the West Indies Federation. Sir Grantley Adams became first leader of the West Indies Federation.
Hugh Gordon Cummins serves as Premier of the island until self-government.

The Cabinet system of Government was instituted.

1959 / The first experiment with a common entrance examination to determine entrants to Government Secondary Schools.

1961 / Full internal Self-Government achieved. Errol Barrow becomes the first Prime Minister of Barbados.

1962 / Dissolution of the West Indies Federation.
Free Secondary Education introduced.

1963 / Voting age reduced from 21 to 18 years.

Abolition of fees in Government Secondary Grammar Schools.

1964 / A Senate of 21 appointed members replaced the Legislative Council.

Legislation was passed permitting peaceful picketing.

1966 / Visit of Her Majesty Queen Elizabeth II and H R H the Duke of Edinburgh.
The 'Barbados Independence Order' laid before Parliament.
Independence achieved November 30.
Right Honourable Errol Barrow becomes first Prime Minister.

1967 / In April, the system of Local Government Council was dissolved and replaced by an Interim Commissioner for Local Government.
On May 18, the island's first native Governor-General, Sir Winston Scott, was appointed.
The National Insurance and Social Security Scheme was initiated with the aim of introducing and developing on a phased basis, a comprehensive scheme of social security.

1968 / Caribbean Free Trade Association (CARIFTA) was established May 1, with Antigua,

Barbados, Guyana and Trinidad and Tobago as the founding members. Dominica, Grenada, St Kitts-Nevis-Anguilla, St Lucia and St Vincent joined the Association on July 1, 1968.

1969 / On September 1, all Local Government services were transferred from the interim Commissioner to the Central Government and such statutory bodies as the Sanitation and Cemeteries Board, the National Assistance Board and Parks and Beaches Commission.
The Barbados Development Bank was established.

1971 / The Democratic Labour Party led by the Rt Honourable Errol Barrow won a two-thirds majority in the General Election.
The system of single member constituencies was introduced when the island was divided into 24 electoral districts known as constituencies.

1972 / The Central Bank of Barbados was established by an Act of Parliament.

1973 / Representatives of four independent Commonwealth Caribbean Countries, Guyana, Jamaica, Trinidad and Tobago and Barbados signed a treaty on July 4, establishing the Caribbean Community (CARICOM) on August 1.

1976 / The Barbados Labour Party (BLP) led by J M G M 'Tom' Adams, won a two-thirds majority in the September General Election.

1978 / The Barbados Defence Force was formally established.

1980 / The Representation of the People's (Amendment) Act was passed to increase the number of constituencies from 24 to 27.

1981 / On June 18, the Barbados Labour Party (BLP), led by the Rt Hon Tom Adams as Prime Minister was returned to power.
Hosting of CARIFESTA – the Regional Arts Festival. About 2,000 artists and performers

from 33 Caribbean and Pan-American countries participated.

1982 / April 8-11, the President of the United States, Ronald Reagan and Mrs Reagan paid an official visit to Barbados. This occasion marked the first visit, while in office, of a United States President.

1983 / Barbados played a pivotal role in the US-led intervention in Grenada after the October coup.

1985 / On March 11, the Prime Minister, the Rt Hon Tom Adams died.

Harold Bernard 'Bree' St John sworn in as the country's new Prime Minister.

1986 / On May 25, the Democratic Labour Party won 24 of the 27 seats contested in the General Elections.

1987 / On June 1, the Prime Minister, the Rt Hon Errol Walton Barrow died.

Lloyd Erskine Sandiford sworn in as the country's new Prime Minister.

1989 / Barbados celebrated 350 years of unbroken parliamentary rule in June.

1990 / Dame Nita Barrow became the island's first female Governor-General on June 6.

Electoral and Boundaries Commission Review of Boundaries Order to increase the number of seats in the House of Assembly from 27 to 28.

Order comes into effect with dissolution of Parliament on December 29, 1990.

1991 / The Democratic Labour Party, led by Prime Minister Erskine Sandiford was returned to Office on January 22.

1993 / Owen Arthur was appointed Leader of the Opposition following the resignation of the party leader, Henry Forde in July.

1994 / The Barbados Labour Party, led by Owen Arthur won 19 of the 28 seats contested in the General Election.

1996 / Sir Clifford Straughn Husbands, GCMG, KA, became the sixth Governor-General of Barbados on June 1.

1997 / President Clinton's visit: the President of the United States and Mrs Clinton paid an official visit to Barbados. The year also marked the signing of the Martime Agreement between Barbados and the United States.

The inauguration of the 1st Emancipation Day, August 1.

1998 / The inauguration of the National Heroes' Day, April 28.

President Fidel Castro's visit: the President of the Republica of Cuba visited Barbados and participated in the emancipation day celebrations and unveiled a plaque commemorating the lives of those who died in the Cubana airline crash of 1976.

1999 / The Barbados Labour Party, led by Rt Hon Owen Arthur, won 26 of the 28 seats contested in the General Election on January 20.

2000 / Barbados wins its first individual Olympic medal as Obadele Thompson captures bronze in the 100 metres final, in Sydney, Australia in September.

2003 / The Barbados Labour Party, led by Rt Hon Owen Arthur, won 23 of the 30 seats contested in the General Election on May 21.

2005 / The Glendiary Prison severely damaged by fire after prison riots in March.

Kensington Oval demolished in preparation for Cricket World Cup 2007.

/ Marcia Manning

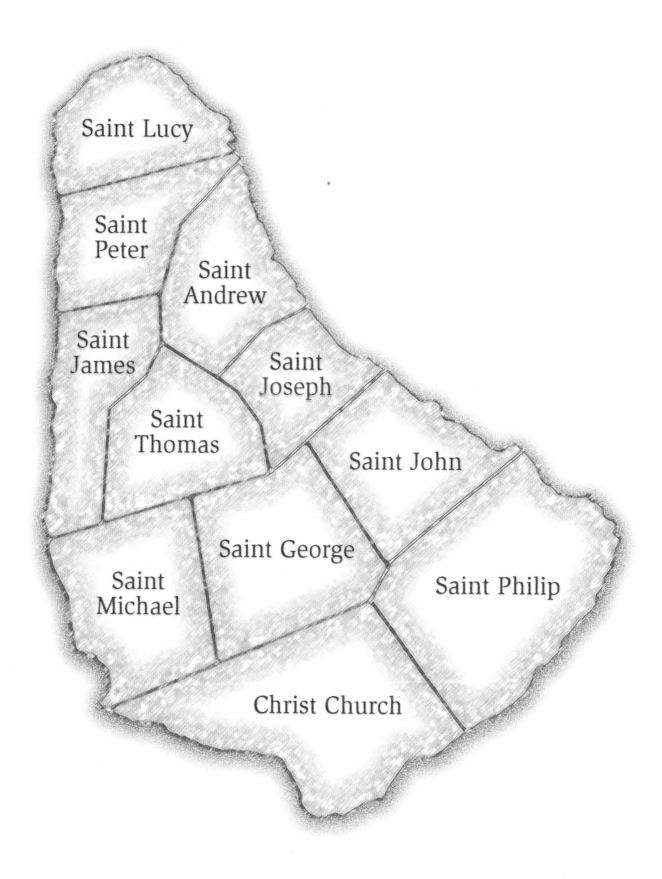

The Parishes

The parishes of Barbados have been an integral part of its identity for hundreds of years.

The island was divided into six parishes in 1629, just two years after the first English settlers arrived. In the 1640s these were revised to form 11 parishes upon which the local government system was anchored, with the vestry, made up of 16-elected property owners in each parish, empowered to collect taxes and rents to spend on basic facilities. The centre point of each parish was its church, which had an important social and political role.

The system remained in operation until 1969, when central government took over their role. However, the parishes are still a source of pride for the inhabitants of each and are constantly used as a guide to location on the island.

Bruce Hemming

Christ Church

NESTLED between metropolitan Saint Michael in the west and rugged Saint Philip in the east, Christ Church is the island's **most southern parish**. With an area of just about 60 sq kilometres and a population of 53,000, the primarily residential area is also the home of the **Grantley Adams International Airport**. Lush agricultural land and a vibrant fishing community are also some of Christ Church's features.

Oistins, one of four towns on Barbados, has a long-standing tradition as the island's major fishing port and is a popular venue for night-time entertainment. The glowing flames of outdoor kitchens and the rhythmic sounds of indigenous music beckon both visitors and locals to this authentically Caribbean dining experience. The culinary and cultural adventure is often heightened during the Easter weekend when the annual **Oistins Fish Festival** transforms the small town into a hub of celebration in art, craft, cuisine and performance.

Standing atop **Oistins Hill** is the historic **Christ Church Parish Church**. The building, erected in 1935, is the fourth to be constructed on the historic property. The church, which is best known as the locus of the Anglican religion in southern Barbados, is also famous for the Chase Vault. Legendary tales of the coffins in the family tomb mysteriously shifting on their own continue to have a place in Barbadian folklore.

Indisputably, Christ Church's beaches are one of its most prominent features. Skirting most of the parish's perimeter, the mostly placid waters are a popular tourist attraction. From the surfing-suited waves at **Silver Sands** to the swimmer's delight at **Accra**, Christ Church finds continued favour with beach-loving tourists and locals.

Visitors to Christ Church will also find a hive of activity at **Saint Lawrence Gap**. The strip, which is the centre of nightlife on the South Coast, is well known for its multicultural and traditional Bajan cuisine, live band entertainment, bars and clubs.

Other must-see attractions dotting the parish include the **Graeme Hall Nature Sanctuary** – a haven for exotic species of flora and fauna; **South Point Lighthouse** – a historic signal for marine navigation of yore; **Ocean Park** – the island's aquarium and the **Barbados Golf Club** – the sport's southern putting Mecca.

above & middle / Ocean Park

top / Graeme Hall Nature Sanctuary

opposite / Oistins beach

Bruce Hemming

Bruce Hemming

above / Ocean Park is a unique Marine Aquarium bringing the spectacular underwater world of Barbados and the Caribbean to visitors without having to get wet! It is a great day out for couples, singles or the entire family offering a new interactive feeding station, a relaxing park atmosphere, a kids playground, the 'Shark Bites' restaurant and bar, the 'Something Fishy' souvenir shop and, of course, Pirate Adventure mini golf

left / Christchurch Parish Church

opposite top / Rockley Beach

opposite bottom / the Barbados Golf Club, with its 18-hole championship public course is the heart and soul of Barbados golf, being ideal for all abilities. Fanned by south coast breezes, this links-style 6,705-yard par-72 golf course features gently rolling hills, wide open fairways, a large central lake and a series of coral waste bunkers, as well as excellent off-course facilities

Bruce Hemming

Bruce Hemming

Saint Andrew

IN THE northeast of the island, surrounded by rugged terrain and skirted by the turbulent Atlantic Ocean, Saint Andrew is a parish of unspoiled beauty. With a population of around 5,700, this chiefly residential and agricultural parish is the sixth largest of Barbados' 11 parishes.

In this clayey 32 sq kilometre section of the island, the country's highest point towers above the foamy currents of the surrounding beaches. **Mount Hillaby**, standing at 333 metres above sea level, is a reputed sightseeing point for breathtaking views of the island's coastline.

With its distinguished landscape of clay and sandstones – a rarity for the mostly coral limestone-covered island – Saint Andrew is home to the island's lone pottery village. **The Chalky Mount** community, known by many as 'The Potteries', has roots dating back to the 18th century. The district is recognised as one of Barbados' most authentic locations for clay craft where the artisans' trade secrets have survived for generations.

Morgan Lewis Mill is another one of Saint Andrew's premier historic features. The only functioning sugar mill on the island takes visitors on a journey to the days when 'sugar was King' in Barbados. Complete with all the trappings of a historic sugar refinery, the Barbados National Trust-restored property offers a complete exhibition of the island's sugar cane production past. In addition, Governor General of the island, His Excellency, **Sir Clifford Straughn Husbands**, GCMG, KA, was born on the surrounding Morgan Lewis Plantation in 1926.

Other ecological features in Saint Andrew include the uninhabited **Turner's Hall Woods**, the recreational area at **Barclays Park**, and **Green Pond** and **Long Pond**, which run along the northeast coast. **Ermy Bourne Highway** is also becoming a famed area in Saint Andrew. The highway was nicknamed 'Calypso Bowl' after becoming the main venue for the **Party Monarch finals** during the annual **Crop Over Festival**.

above / the avenue of mahogany trees leading to Cherry Tree Hill

top / picnickers at Barclays Park

opposite / the Morgan Lewis Mill

overleaf / view of the east coast and the Chalky Mount

Bruce Hemming

above / the lion at Gun Hill Signal Station

Saint George

THE second largest of the island's parishes, Saint George is 45 sq kilometres
and provides residential dwelling for 19,000 Barbadians. With its central
location, it is one of only two parishes untouched by the ocean – the other
being Saint Thomas.

Apart from being the home of Bajans, Saint George is also known for its green,
rolling fields of sugar cane. In addition, the **Saint George Valley** is a major
geographical feature of the island, separating the main coral limestone terraces
that cross the island from a lower ridge in Christ Church.

The **Gun Hill Signal Station** also finds its home in the central parish. This
historic military landmark, built in 1818, once played a pivotal role in the
English colony's signal station system, which alerted officials of approaching
vessels. In addition, this location has become a favoured spot for capturing
breathtaking views of the southern areas of Barbados.

Accompanying the signal station at Gun Hill is the monumental and stately
white lion, perched on a grassy slope just below the stately military tower.
The sculpture, which was carved out of a single rock and completed in 1868,
is thought to be the handiwork of a British soldier on duty at the station
during colonial days. The lion masterpiece measures three metres tall and five
metres wide.

Francia Plantation House is another must-see relic in Saint George. Its
beautifully landscaped terraces and lawns complement a fascinating collection
of Barbadian antiques, china, silverware, and maps of olden Barbados. The
Brazilian panelling of the history-filled great house interior also makes it one of
Saint George's best kept treasures.

In addition, **Saint George Parish Church** adds to the parish's historic inventory.
The church, rebuilt in 1784 after destruction by fire, is the oldest ecclesiastical
architectural landmark in Barbados. It also houses 'Rise to Power' by Benjamin
West, RA, the famed artist whose work also hangs in Buckingham Palace.

Bruce Hemming

Saint James

THE WEST COAST, with its signature golden sands, marks the location of Saint James. This parish, best known for its long stretch of tourist accommodation along its beach-lined fringe, is also home to 25,000 Barbadians. In addition, several historic landmarks abound on this 34 sq kilometre section of the island.

Holetown, originally called Jamestown, is one of the island's four towns. Additionally, it is the site of the **first English landing** on Barbados by the crew of the *Olive Blossom* in 1625. Today, an **obelisk-shaped monument** marks the settlement, which was initially named after the island's primary benefactor, King James I.

Just moments away from the epochal location, **Saint James Parish Church** also has its boast in Barbados' annals. Erected in 1847, it is among the island's four oldest churches. In addition, the Anglican church is outfitted with a bell on which the words, 'God Bless King William, 1696' are inscribed. This relic predates similar tolling wonders in the Western Hemisphere, including the Liberty Bell in Pennsylvania, USA.

Saint James' **beaches** are among its most distinguished features. Visitors and locals relish in the tranquil surf in this section of the island and consider it a popular venue for sea-bathing and beachside relaxation. However, the parish is also a wonder **underwater**. Facilities for snorkelling, scuba and other undersea exploration dot the surrounding coast.

In keeping with its tradition of tourist attractions, the parish is an ideal location for restaurant dining where a variety of international and traditional cuisine is delivered to eager epicurean fans. In addition, sports and shopping facilities abound in Saint James. **Four golf courses** are a part of the parish's leisure offering – three at **Sandy Lane** and one at **Royal Westmoreland**. This famed golf parish is hosting the 2006 World Golf Championships-World Cup and the site of Tiger Woods' wedding to Elin Nordegren in 2004.

Bruce Hemming

above / Paynes Bay

opposite / snorkelling at Folkestone Marine Reserve

previous page / Sandy Lane beach

Bruce Hemming

Bruce Hemming

above / the Holetown Monument, marking the place of the first English settlement

left / tourists enjoying a catamaran trip off the coast of Saint James

opposite top / the magnificent golf course, centrepiece of the Royal Westmoreland estate, was given recently the accolade of being ranked number 31 among the world's best courses outside the USA by *Golf Digest* and recommendations do not come any better than that. Winning Ryder Cup captain Ian Woosnam, a homeowner at Westmoreland, says the four par 3s are some of the best he has played anywhere in the world

opposite bottom / Saint James Parish Church

Bruce Hemming

Willie Alleyne

Willie Alleyne

Saint John

IN THE eastern part of Barbados, this parish boasts a coastline of **fishing bays** and an intriguing, rich history. Saint John's 35 sq kilometre area is the home of around 9,500 Barbadians and a pair of the island's most well-known religious landmarks.

Codrington College, the oldest theological seminary in the Western Hemisphere, overlooks the Atlantic Ocean from its stately location on one of the parish's hills. Opened in 1745, the historic facility is the product of a generous endowment by Christopher Codrington. The benefactor bequeathed the property to the Society for the Propagation of the Gospel – an Anglican mission agency established to ensure the spiritual vitality of the Church of England in the Western Hemisphere during the 18th century. Today, it is one of the region's chief learning centres for aspiring clergymen. Moreover, it ranks as one of the island's most elegant architectural treasures.

Saint John's Church – built in 1836 – is the parish's other ecclesiastical jewel. The church occupies the edge of a cliff, making it a perfect spot for sightseers who often trek to the historic location to enjoy a panoramic view of the East Coast. Beyond scenery, the church is also famed for its fine architecture and interior. The remains of **Ferdinando Paleologus**, a descendant of Emperor Constantine the Great, who died in 1678, are also buried in the church cemetery.

The small fishing vessels and nets clustered along the coast also tell of Saint John's rich seafaring culture. From **Conset Bay** to **Martin's Bay**, many eastern fisher folk ply their trade here at sea and on land. Away from the bustle of city life, these tranquil areas that open to the ocean are postcard-worthy images of idyllic Barbados.

Also, both visitors and locals enjoy the recreational options that Saint John offers, including the beach at **Bath** – the parish's treat to swimmers and picnickers, with its park benches, playground and shady trees.

above / Saint Margaret's Church, another well-known in Saint John

top & opposite / Codrington College – the oldest theological seminary in the Western Hemisphere

Bruce Hemming

Bruce Hemming

Saint Joseph

THIS parish is renowned far and wide as the home of the 'Soup Bowl', Andromeda Gardens and the Flower Forest. Not only does Saint Joseph boast such natural attractions, but it is also a residential location with 7,500 Bajans living throughout its 27 sq kilometre area.

Bathsheba, a popular sightseeing spot, is a tranquil district on the island's eastern countryside. In addition, it is the home of several international surfing competitions. Nicknamed the 'Soup Bowl' for its surf and phenomenal waves, which beckon eager surfers worldwide, the beach at Bathsheba is a long-standing part of the Bajan sightseeing inventory. Many visitors and locals rank this community, with its lookout to the Atlantic Ocean and green lawns, as a picnic-perfect spot. In addition, Bathsheba is known for its signature boulders that ornament the shore and shoot up from the frothy sea.

In addition to ocean beauty, Saint Joseph boasts a wide collection of flora and fauna. At **Andromeda Gardens**, for example, horticulture is at its best. Six acres of exotic species and other traditional blooms perched atop a cliff are some of the features that lure visitors to this fascinating landscape. The **Flower Forest** is a similar attraction, which adds a nature trail to its botanical gardens theme. The lush, green lawns and its 50-acre expanse covered with palms and other tropical plants make it a picturesque place of interest. In addition, the Forest offers views of the East Coast and the surrounding rugged terrain from its location 850 feet above sea level.

Like many parishes across Barbados, historic landmarks evidence the influence of the British. In Saint Joseph, **Cotton Tower** marks the island's centuries-old colonial past. This military landmark represents one of the nation's strategies in fending off enemy attacks. Cotton Tower, a 19th century signal station, is preserved by the Barbados National Trust and is open for public viewing.

above & top / a four-wheel-drive trip up to Edge Cliff rewards with magnificent views

opposite / the Round House

previous page / the beach and iconic rock formations of Bathsheba

Willie Alleyne

above / view of Scotland District from the Flower Forest

left / Cotton Tower Signal Station

opposite / the Flower Forest

Willie Alleyne

Willie Alleyne

Bruce Hemming

Saint Lucy

NEARLY 10,000 Barbadians have found a home in this 35 sq kilometre parish. At the **northernmost tip** of Barbados, Saint Lucy rounds off the island just beyond the hotel-dotted golden sands of the West Coast.

Cliffs and rocky landforms run around most of Saint Lucy's perimeter, offering themselves for a beating by the seething waters of the Atlantic Ocean. However, towards the western side of the parish, the rough waters give way to more placid **swimmer-friendly seas**.

One of the island's most intriguing attractions is also based in Saint Lucy. **The Animal Flower Cave** is a wonder of rock pools and sea anemones with its naturally-formed 'windows' to the sea. The spectacular views it offers of the pounding surf and its water-filled chambers make it a must-see Bajan attraction.

Saint Lucy's historic contributions to Barbados are also invaluable. **Errol Walton Barrow**, often called Barbados' Father of Independence, was born there in 1920. After being elected Premier of the island in 1961, he ushered Barbados into independence from England in 1966 and became the first Prime Minister of the country. He is one of the island's officially appointed National Heroes and holds historic recognition for his introduction of a National Insurance and Social Security program. Barrow, who died in 1987, is remembered by a national holiday named in his honour and he is pictured on the B$50 bill.

above / the late Errol Barrow, Father of Independence, was born in Saint Lucy

top / the prized black belly sheep

opposite / Cove Bay

The Saint Lucy Parish Church is one of the parish's historic landmarks. The church building – the fourth to stand on the site – was built in 1837 after nearly two centuries of rebuilding projects.

Saint Lucy has established itself as a prime location for experiencing the tranquillity of the Barbados countryside and its natural wonders. With its lush fields, rugged cliffs and ocean-lined fringes, it emerges as an ideal example of rural living on the island.

Bruce Hemming

Bruce Hemming

above / Cove Bay

left / a chattel house

opposite top / tourists arriving by four-wheel drive trucks on a trip to Cove Bay

opposite bottom / the famous Animal Flower Caves

Bruce Hemming

Willie Alleyne

Willie Alleyne

Saint Michael

AS THE home of **Bridgetown**, the capital of Barbados, Saint Michael features myriad historic landmarks, a rich heritage and a bustling commercial district. In addition to being the island's metropolis, it is a densely populated residential parish with an area of 38 sq kilometres.

The parish is not only the location for many island landmarks, but it is also the home of many of the island's iconic citizens. For example, the cricketing greats who form the famous **Three Ws, Sir Everton Weekes, Sir Frank Worrell and Sir Clyde Walcott,** all claim the parish as their hometown. In addition, **Sir Garfield Sobers,** hailed as the world's most prolific cricket all-rounder was born in the Bayland community just outside Bridgetown.

Nearby the cricketing legend's birthplace, the island's most fascinating historic locations are still intact. **The Garrison Historic Area** houses the **Barbados Museum,** an old military detention barracks; **Saint Ann's Fort**, the old headquarters for the British military and the **Garrison Savannah**, the island's historic horseracing hub. St Michael is also home to Barbados' main port of entry by sea, **Bridgetown Port**.

In Bridgetown, symbols of the colonial past dot the landscape. **Queen's Park**, the former residence of the General of British troops in the West Indies, now doubles as a recreational facility and a historic landmark. In the **Heroes' Square** area, **Lord Nelson's Bronze Statue**, the fountain commemorating the beginning of a piped water service in Bridgetown, and The Public Buildings – housing the third **oldest Parliament in the Commonwealth,** make Bridgetown a historic haven.

In addition, a strong religious heritage is evident in the city area. Several Anglican churches surround Bridgetown, with two – **Saint Mary's Church** and the **Saint Michael Cathedral** – in the heart of the busy town. In addition, the **Jewish Synagogue** stands just beyond the main streets of Bridgetown and marks nearly 400 years of Judaic traditions in Barbados.

There are two main rum distilleries on the island; the Rum Refinery of **Mount Gay** Limited and the West Indies Rum Distillery (producers of **Cockspur**) are both located in Saint Michael.

In addition to serving as the location of some of the island's most celebrated landmarks, Saint Michael is also known for its shopping facilities, while its outdoor dining in areas such as **Baxter's Road** and the popular nightlife area at **Bay Street** are some of the parish's contemporary features.

above / the Swing Bridge in Bridgetown

top / racing at the Garrison Savannah

middle / a tour at the Mount Gay Rum distillery

opposite / the dolphin fountain in Heroes' Square, Bridgetown

Willie Alleyne

Willie Alleyne

above / an old-style residence in Bridgetown

top / a cruise ship arrives at Bridgetown Port

left / historic buildings at the Garrison Savannah area

opposite top / a house in Bay Street

opposite bottom / one of the newer developments in Bridgetown

Willie Alleyne

Willie Alleyne

Willie Alleyne

Bruce Hemming

Saint Peter

LOCATED in the northwestern part of the island, Saint Peter is just over 30 sq kilometres in area. Skirted by **sandy beaches** and dotted with tourist accommodation along its coast, Saint Peter is also the home of nearly 11,500 Barbadians.

In addition, Saint Peter is the location for many of the island's prime attractions. **Farley Hill National Park**, with its clusters of tall trees and splendid views of the East Coast, is one of best-known recreational spots in Barbados. In addition, it is the venue for some of the island's main events, including the **Barbados Jazz Festival** – the Caribbean's finest celebration of the genre. The **old mansion** standing on Farley Hill's grounds is another one of Saint Peter's treasures. **Sir Graham Briggs** erected the edifice in preparation for the visit of Prince Alfred, Duke of Edinburgh, in 1861. Before it was destroyed by fire in 1965, it was also the included in scenes from the motion picture, *Island in the Sun*.

Saint Peter is also the location of **Speightstown**, Barbados' second largest town. The tiny commercial hub, named after **William Speight**, a member of Governor Hawley's British government in 1639, had previously acquired the name, 'Little Bristol'. Apparently, with its bustling sugar production traffic, it displayed an intensity of vigour strikingly close to that of the British metropolis. Today, Speightstown maintains a vibrant fishing culture and is the site of a small shopping district.

While locals may feel at home in the northern parish, it is also the preferred residence for non-Barbadians. For example, **Claudette Colbert**, actress of *Cleopatra* fame, chose Speightstown as her home and retired from her on-screen career there. Just minutes away from Colbert's former residence, the **Port St Charles Marina**, a luxury residential development, is a cluster of villas mostly occupied by visitors intrigued by the Barbados beachfront.

Saint Peter is one of Barbados' finest offerings in history, sightseeing and luxury living. It is also the home of **St Nicholas Abbey**, a property that dates back to 1650, believed to be the **oldest house in Barbados**.

above / US singer and songwriter Jill Scott, performing at the Barbados Jazz Festival

top / parrots at the Barbados Wildlife Reserve

opposite / Farley Hill National Park

above / Built in 1650, St Nicholas Abbey is one of just three Jacobean Mansions existing in the Western Hemisphere. It remains much as it has for the previous three centuries, preserving history and traditions in the production of sugar and rum since the late 17th century.

left / the Port St Charles Marina

opposite top / the famous Mullins Bay

opposite bottom / a typical street in Speightstown

Bruce Hemming

Bruce Hemming

Bruce Hemming

Willie Alleyne

Saint Philip

SHARING the title of 'Largest Parish' with Christ Church, Saint Philip is Barbados' southeast gem. It is home for 26,000 Barbadians and provides a comfortable combination of suburban and rural living. In addition, the parish shares its 61 sq kilometre area with some of the island's most prized historic and leisure landmarks.

Sam Lord's Castle – an 1820s mansion with its antique furnishings – stands on the property adjacent to one of Saint Philip's many coastal lookouts to the Atlantic Ocean. The Georgian house, built by famed seafarer, **Samuel Hall Lord**, is one of the parish's most legendary locations. Tales of the buccaneer-owner's trickery in wrecking ships, whose crews were in search of the island's main seaport, are still a part of Barbadian folklore. In addition to being a landmark rich in history, Sam Lord's Castle was also the main filming location for 1996 episodes of *Bold and Beautiful*, the popular American daytime soap opera.

Saint Philip's place in Barbados' history is also grounded at **Sunbury Plantation House**. The centuries-old plantation building is one of the island's most accurate impressions of a traditional sugar estate great house. The building, with its original furnishings, antique prints and collection of horse-drawn carriages, is a must-see on any visitor's sightseeing slate. In addition, its popularity as a wedding and special events venue is growing among locals and visitors alike.

Ragged Point, the **most easterly point** on the island, is another one of Saint Philip's features. The **East Point lighthouse**, one of four on the island, also stands on this section of the parish. It is well known for its breathtaking views of the island's entire East Coast and some of the northern points. In addition, not far away is **Culpepper Island**, a small landform, which extends from the island's mainland.

Saint Philip also finds favour as the sea-bather's delight. **Crane Beach** is one of the parish's several beaches, and the setting for Barbados' first-ever resort hotel, **The Crane**. Farther along the coast, however, rougher waters forbid swimmers and inexperienced surfers from venturing into the Atlantic's turbulent surf.

above / drilling for oil – first struck in the Woodbourne area in 1966

opposite / the cliffs overlooking Crane beach

above & left / set in the heart of tranquil St Philip countryside, Sunbury is a superb example of a 300-year old Barbadian Sugar Estate Great House. It features mahogany antiques, old prints and a unique collection of horse drawn carriages in the spacious grounds. Guided tours and full catering services, including weddings, are offered at Sunbury

opposite top / Sam Lord's Castle

opposite bottom / the Crane Resort

Bruce Hemming

Willie Alleyne

Willie Alleyne

Willie Alleyne

Saint Thomas

THIS central parish boasts no coastal surf or splendid beachfront sunsets; however, it is one of Barbados' most treasured parishes. The fifth largest parish on the island, Saint Thomas is chiefly a residential parish, with 13,000 of Barbados' population living there.

In addition, Saint Thomas is the location of **Harrison's Cave** – the only cave of its kind in the world, where running water shares a space with coloured crystal-like formations. In addition to being the cave explorer's delight, it is also one of the island's premier attractions. A tram-driven tour through the underground network of lakes, streams, and waterfalls, coupled with moments of on-foot exploration, add to the Harrison's Cave experience.

On the neighbouring property, another of Saint Thomas' attractions – **Welchman Hall Gully** – is well known for its relaxing properties. The gully, about 1.2 kilometres long, takes on the characteristics of a tropical nature trail. The exotic species growing there include nutmeg, bamboo and a variety of palms. In addition, its lush landscape, rare fruit trees and the agile monkeys, which have found a home here, accentuate its untouched beauty. Welchman Hall Gully also features a **cave with an enormous pillar** formed from the joining of a stalactite (rock formation that hangs from the ceiling) and a stalagmite (rock formation that grows from the ground) over time. With a 1.2-metre diameter, the formation is one of the oldest in the world.

The **Springvale Eco-Heritage Museum** is also located adjacent to the gully. This conservatory, dedicated to showcasing Barbados of yore, takes visitors along the path of a 200-acre plantation. Aside from viewing the main aspects of the traditional Bajan living experience, a nature trail that winds through fields, towering coconut trees and beds of planted vegetables provides a one-of-a-kind look at undeveloped Barbados.

Earthworks Pottery is also nestled in the central nooks of Saint Thomas. Tours of the studio enable fans of sculpture and clay craft to get a firsthand look at a pottery, while craftspeople work steadily at creating new works of art. The Pottery also features a gallery displaying Bajans' handiwork.

above / an example of the pottery produced by Earthworks Pottery. Founded in the mid-1970s as a project designed to revive the tradition of pottery-making in Barbados, Earthworks evolved into a cooperative during the 1980s when several independent potters shared costs in a small studio. It now continues to create functional works of art with a passion and a unique Bajan style. Here you can buy anything from the smallest custom-made piece to a full hand-made, hand-decorated dinnerware service, all shipped to your home on completion. Thay have received many awards, including the Ernst and Young Entrepreneur of the Year. Located in the heart of Barbados, the studio is beautifully decorated with mosaics on the outside. Also on site is the Tulis Batik studio producing quality batiks while you watch

opposite / Welchman Hall Gully

The Parishes / *Sueann Tannis*

Willie Alleyne

Bruce Hemming

Willie Alleyne

above & right / Harrison's Cave

opposite top / Welchman Hall Gully

opposite bottom / a view of Lion Castle Polo Estate, a luxury property development in Saint Thomas, centred around a world-class polo field

Willie Alleyne

Willie Alleyne

above & right / Harrison's Cave

opposite top / Welchman Hall Gully

opposite bottom / a view of Lion Castle Polo Estate, a luxury property development in Saint Thomas, centred around a world-class polo field

Willie Alleyne

A Cultural Overview

above, top & opposite |
participants in the island's annual
Crop Over festival

BARBADIAN culture is a product of adaptation and evolution. With a colonial period dominated solely by Britain and the mass of its population deriving from Africa, Barbados evolved a system of beliefs, values, customs, behaviours and artefacts that is primarily a blend of only two worlds. A distinctly **creolised**, but not totally homogenous, culture is the result.

Racial prejudice is not overt, and the population lives in relative harmony, but the plantation slavery system has left its mark on the Barbados psyche. Family structure tends to be matriarchal, without the presence of a constant male. Females increasingly trump the males in education, ambition and responsibility. Gender and family relations are therefore somewhat fractious.

Currently the ethnic mix is 90 per cent of African or African-mixed descent, four per cent white, and six per cent other (primarily Indian and Chinese). Among the whites are a growing number of expatriates from Britain, the rest of Europe and North America. In winter the population swells with wealthy holiday homeowners.

The influx of tourists has had its inevitable impact, as locals endeavour to meet their tastes for products, services, accommodation and entertainment. The influence of America is asserted through music and TV, a fact that is often cited in complaints about the way Barbadian behaviour and consumption patterns have changed in modern times.

All of these factors continue to shape Barbados' cultural landscape. What then is authentic here? Constant adaptation.

There is increasing recognition of culture's contribution to economic development and a sense of national identity. Thus, the Barbados government

encourages, develops and promotes cultural goods and services through numerous institutions.

The primary one is the **National Cultural Foundation**. The NCF has been responsible for two major festivals, NIFCA (National Independence Festival of Creative Arts) and (until 2007) Crop Over. In between festivals, the NCF organises training sessions, seminars, exhibitions and events for the visual, literary and performing arts.

Heritage

The island's history, economy and lifestyles can be read in its architecture and housing patterns. Thankfully, the **Barbados National Trust** has been able to help preserve some of the island's historic buildings.

Whether the plantation is working or carved up, many of their houses still stand. So do charming wooden **chattel houses**, so named because they could be disassembled and moved as the owners' chattel. Both are adapted to tropical conditions. Window hoods give shelter from rain or blazing sun. Parapetted, hipped, and high-peaked roofs withstand fierce winds, as do shutters. Jalousies allow regulated airflow.

Built in the 19th century for the British naval forces of this area and now a historic district, **St Anne's Garrison** provides other fine examples of architectural heritage. At its edge is the 18th century **Bush Hill House**, where **George Washington** spent several weeks.

In early 20th century, when plantations were being sold off in parcels, remittance money enabled many thrifty Bajans to purchase land. Growing families carved up these pieces further, so that in any village you would find tiny, crowded houses, and dozens of related people looking after each other's children and old folk. Yards were used to rear livestock and poultry, and grow bananas, vegetables and herbs. These extended family 'islands within the island' reinforced an already insular mentality.

The architecture of the 20th century shows the growth of a pragmatic middle class. Professional people tend to live in the 'heights and terraces', while the average Barbadian lives in rural communities or the greater Bridgetown area. Lately, there has been less inhibition in the use of colour on buildings.

Religion

Barbados prides itself in being religious. **Anglicans** account for 40 per cent. Other Protestant faiths, including **Methodists**, **Moravians** and **Pentecostals**, account for 27 per cent, and **Roman Catholics** for 4 per cent.

Some 12 per cent of the population refer to themselves as 'other', which includes **Muslims**, **Hindus**, **Jews**, **Rastafarians** and **Spiritual Baptists**, whose church originated here in 1957. Members of this sect dress colourfully for their

above / the Bridgetown Synagogue

top / a chattel house

middle / the Jumma Mosque on Kensington New Road, Bridgetown

opposite top / St Patrick's Roman Catholic Cathedral, Bay Street, Saint Michael

opposite bottom / St Michael's Anglican Cathedral, Bridgetown

lively ceremonies, which incorporate African ancestral beliefs. However, a full 17 per cent of Barbadians identify themselves as affiliated to no religion, which is surprising in a context where schooldays, some affairs of state, and many other gatherings begin with prayer. Women vastly outnumber men in church.

Local Food and Drink

Next to church (sometimes literally) the rum shop is the most enduring social institution of Barbados. There is at least one in every village, where they often do double duty as 'the shop', supplying basic household necessities and foodstuffs. Away from the pressures of work or domestic life, men gather in these locales to relax, gossip, and express their views.

Rum, which was invented in Barbados over 300 years ago, continues to be made here and is consumed in large quantities.

Sorrel, a spiced red beverage made from the sepals of a shrub, is popular especially around Christmas. **Mauby** is made by boiling the bark of another tropical shrub with various spices and liberal amounts of sweetener to counteract its bitterness. The mauby seller was once an iconic figure in Barbados, carrying a vat of the liquid on her head, dispensing it from a spigot into a glass.

Delicious drinks are also made from local fruits. **Coconut water**, from the green nut, is available at roadside stands. It efficiently replaces electrolytes lost through sweating in the heat.

The Barbadian palate favours heavy food, high seasoning, and sweet drinks. Although fast food outlets and foreign delicacies in supermarkets have made inroads, most homes and many restaurants serve a traditional menu. Sunday lunch is a big meal, where extended families bond on a regular basis.

Flying fish and **cou-cou** (cornmeal with okras,) is the national dish. **Salt fish** may be substituted. Salt fish is also used to make fish cakes. The consumption of **chicken** per capita would put Barbados high on a global scale! Root vegetables like **eddoes**, **yams** and **sweet potatoes** are grown locally and are very nutritious. **Breadfruit** is another common starchy staple.

In any form, **pork** is held in high esteem. Saturday is the main day for **pudding and souse**. Boiled meat from pig heads and trotters is soused by soaking it in lime juice with onions, grated cucumber and seasoning. Pudding is a form of sausage made chiefly from grated sweet potato.

Whether raised on farms or in backyards, the prized Barbadian **black belly sheep** is the source of lamb for stews and chops.

Fish is increasing in popularity but declining in supply. **Fish fries** are popular on weekends, with Oistins being the largest.

Hot peppers and fresh herbs, especially thyme, marjoram and green onion or chives, are essential to Barbadian cuisine. '**Bajan seasoning**' consists of the above seasonings and more. **Pepper sauce** is another essential.

above / a black belly sheep

top / pudding and souse – a Barbadian speciality

middle / fresh tropical fruits – the staple ingredient for a great cocktail

opposite top / the National Cultural Foundation of Barbados, seen here staging a play, is the national agency for the preservation, development and promotion of culture. The NCF also stages the two largest festivals on Barbados' cultural calendar: Crop Over and the National Independence Festival of Creative Arts. Truly, there is always something exciting happening at the NCF

opposite bottom / a rum shop

Mount Gay: the oldest rum in the world

MOUNT GAY has been synonymous with rum making for over 300 years. The earliest surviving written evidence of rum production on the Mount Gay estate, in the parish of St Lucy in Barbados, is found in a legal document in the island's archives, dated February 20, 1703. It outlines property and the equipment essential for rum making that was found there: *"two stone windmills... one boiling house with seven coppers, one curing house and one still house"*. This confirms that rum production was already well under way by 1703 making Mount Gay Rum not only the oldest rum in Barbados but also the oldest rum in the world.

Making Mount Gay Rum

The whole process starts amidst the lush, green fields of the island's high quality sugar cane. After planting, the young canes take 12-18 months to mature and are harvested when the sugar content reaches its peak. The cane is taken to a sugar refinery, where the juice is squeezed from the sugar cane fibres and heated to produce sugar crystals. At Mount Gay, molasses, a by-product of sugar refining, is mixed with pure Barbados water and fermented to become alcohol – the start of the rum-making process.

This alcoholic base is distilled carefully and then double distilled to produce two distinctly different types of spirit. A rich, full double-distilled spirit results from the traditional copper pot stills, which have been used since the 1700s. The modern 'Coffey still' produces a more neutral, single-distilled spirit. These two spirits are aged for several years in specially imported Kentucky oak barrels before they are blended to achieve the inimitable flavour of Mount Gay Rums.

When ageing is complete, the single and double distilled spirits are 'married' by the master blender, with an art and skill that has been handed down with care from generation to generation for over 300 years.

International Success

Today Mount Gay Rum is exported to 66 countries worldwide. A favourite of yachtsmen everywhere, Mount Gay sponsors over 100 sailing regattas around the world – in America, Europe, Asia, Australia and the Caribbean. Its global recognition and appreciation is growing each year. Mount Gay's Extra Old and Eclipse rums have both won gold medals and top honours at the most prestigious international competitions.

The Mount Gay Rum Tour

The Mount Gay Visitor's Centre, conveniently located on the Spring Garden Highway just five minutes from the Bridgetown Port, offers visitors 'A Tour Through The History Of The World's Oldest Rum'. Mount Gay is an integral part of the culture, history and the fun of the island; this tour is a Barbadian experience that should not be missed! There is also a gift shop brim full of Mount Gay branded souvenir items and, of course, the best selection of famous Mount Gay Rums in the world.

Seasonal treats include **conkies**, a sweet, spiced mixture of Indian corn or cornmeal, sweet potato, coconut and pumpkin steamed in banana leaf, and **jug-jug,** a savoury sludge made primarily from pigeon peas and salt meat. The rich, fruity and alcoholic 'great cake' or **black cake** is also popular. Traditional sweets are **tamarind balls**, **sugar cakes** (a confection made with sugar, grated coconut and essences) and **guava cheese**.

Language, Customs and Pastimes

The official language of Barbados is English. Standard English is taught in school, but **Bajan dialect**, an English-based Creole, is the local idiom. Bajan dialect arose from a confluence of English with a variety of African languages. Though the tone conveys a lot, the substance can be unintelligible to outsiders. Barbadian speech has a distinctive accent and intonation. When dialect is added and the subject is contentious, the total effect is loud, colourful and often deliberately hilarious. **Stupsing**, a juicy sound made by sucking one's teeth, can indicate emphatic scorn, disbelief or agreement.

Funerals are not simply a ritual for bidding adieu to the deceased, but are important social occasions. It is not uncommon to see women in evening dress at funerals and church services. Prayer and/or the national anthem precede many events. Whoever enters a space is expected to say 'Good morning', or afternoon/evening/night as the case may be; it is impolite to omit this. On the road, courteous Barbadians signal other drivers by flashing headlights or beeping the horn to invite them to make a turn or enter a roadway. A beep-beep in return means 'thank you'. Gossip is a form of currency from which an interesting verb arises – to malicious. Many conversations entail a recital of some branch of the family tree. This is useful to know when gossiping.

At any rum shop or under trees, you are bound to find a group of men 'slamming doms' – playing **dominoes**, slamming down the tiles for emphasis.

Draughts, or checkers, is another popular game, and the several-times world champion, **Suki King**, hails from Barbados.

Warri, a 'pit and pebble' strategy came to Barbados with people of Asante and Yoruba roots. The National Cultural Foundation now makes an effort to keep the knowledge alive.

Beach cricket and **picnics** are popular, cross-generational activities. **Road tennis** originated here and is played in many corners of the island.

Music and Entertainment

Musical groups and choirs include the **Ellerslie Folk Chorale**, the **Barbados National Youth Orchestra** and numerous gospel groups. There are several other school-based orchestras, including some excellent steel pan ones.

There are dozens of well-known singers and musicians. Among the

"On the road, courteous Barbadians signal other drivers by flashing headlights or beeping the horn to invite them to make a turn or enter a roadway. A beep-beep in return means 'thank you'."

top / the Landship – unique to Barbados. This cultural naval dance is accompanied by a tuk band (above)

contemporary icons are: **The Merrymen**; Anthony Carter, the calypsonian, folk singer and now Cultural Ambassador, better known as the **Mighty Gabby**; flannel-voiced veteran **John King**; saxophonist **Arturo Tappin**; and soca idols **Alison Hinds** and **Rupee**. In 2006 a Barbadian teenager known as **Rihanna** ignited the pop charts with a string of international hit records. It is as a top comedic MC that he cannot be overlooked. On steel pans, **David 'Ziggy' Walcott** is currently wowing audiences.

Jazz is becoming increasingly popular, both in concert and club settings.

Dinner theatre revolving around floorshows is popular among tourists, giving singers, musicians and dancers regular employment and a place to shine. **Limbo dancers**, **fire-eaters** and **acrobats** often augment these shows. Fine mimics as well as athletes, the acrobats have a unique speciality act in their repertoire, based on the antics of Barbados' monkeys.

Imitation also forms the basis of cabaret performances by a corps of transvestites or 'female illusionists'. Locals are perhaps not the target audience, with the possible exception of the devotees of **Diva**, whose star turns at the Headliners Calypso Tent have brought down the house since 1999.

The Landship

Unique to Barbados, the Landship is a cultural **dance** that mimics the movements of a ship at sea and of its crew – with a lot of African-derived hip gyrations. Founded in 1837, and modelled on the British navy, Landship members have ranks and titles assigned to them and wear the uniforms of nurses and of naval personnel. The performance includes parades, jigs, hornpipes and maypoles and is accompanied by a **tuk band**, composed of drums, triangle and penny whistle or flute.

Dance, Theatre and the Literary Arts

For both concert spectators and social participants, dancing skill is appreciated. The Pinelands Creative Workshop and the Israel Lovell Foundation support cultural dance with African roots. Backed by polyrhythmic drumming, groups like Dancin' Africa are very popular. There are also two ballet schools, some liturgical dance groups, and a growing number of ballroom and Latin dance schools and groups. Top names are the Barbados Dance Theatre Company and Louise Woodvine.

Theatre tends to focus on broad comedy, historical dramas that seek to illuminate the Caribbean experience, and didactic material concerning such topics as HIV/AIDS or mental illness.

Several theatre people excel in more than one field: Actors **Andrew Pilgrim** and **Varia Williams** are successful lawyers. Playwright **Hilary Beckles'** 'day job' is Pro-Vice Chancellor and Principal of the University of the West Indies, Cave Hill Campus. In addition to being a community worker, writer-director **Winston**

above / acclaimed Bajan author George Lamming

top / 'Vendors' by Barbadian artist Anne Dodson

Farrell is a published and popular poet. The list could go on and on – testimony to the protean talent with which this island is blessed.

Barbadian audiences are tough. They are often reticent to respond, and in the case of serious theatre, can react quite inappropriately. It is little wonder then, that there are fewer dramatic than comedic productions.

Broad comedy is the forte of Barbadian theatre, and the performing seasons of *Pampalam*, *Laff it Off*, and *Bajan Bus Stop* are eagerly awaited yearly. These groups spoof current events and trends, with characters that have become familiar favourites. These productions also travel overseas.

The late poet, dramatist and editor, **Frank Collymore** (1893-1980) set a high standard for the **literary arts** in Barbados. Both he and **Timothy Callender** (1946-1989), who wrote short stories, plays and a novel, helped to gain international exposure for the island's contribution to Caribbean literature.

The National Independence Festival of Creative Arts includes a literary component that gives exposure and cash prizes to winners. Bolstered by the Central Bank, the **Frank Collymore Literary Endowment** also presents substantial annual awards to emerging writers of drama, prose fiction, non-fiction and poetry, whose work could hold its own in any arena.

Established contemporary luminaries include **George Lamming** and **Austin 'Tom' Clarke**, whose novels are internationally acclaimed, and the poet **Edward 'Kamau' Brathwaite**. Notable emerging writers include **Robert Edison Sandiford** and **Linda Deane**. Performance poetry is growing in popularity, with **Deanne Kennedy**, **Winston Farrell** and **Kelly Chase** among the top practitioners.

The Visual Arts

The role of the **visual arts** in Barbados has changed over time. At first, painting was a way of recording the visible elements of local life, and left an intriguing historical legacy. Contemporary Barbadian artists tend to fall into two camps: those who produce work with popular (both local and tourist) taste in mind, and those who explore artistic, personal and social concerns.

Popular painters include **Heather Dawn Scott**, **Fielding Babb**, **Neville Legall**, **Arthur Atkinson** and **Ann Dodson**. Heading the now-established avant-garde are the provocative **Ras Akyem Ramsay** and **Ras Ishi Butcher**, the surrealist **Stanley Greaves** and the spirit-catcher of natural forms, **Alison Chapman-Andrews**. Among the many emerging talents, **Ewan Atkinson** has perhaps had the most impact.

In quantity produced and consumed, sculpture lags far behind painting. The stone-and-ceramicist **Bill Grace** and woodcarver **Wayne 'Onkphra' Wells** are the shining exceptions in this area.

Few artists can sustain themselves with local sales alone. As a result, both decorative and important works have left the island. This is a doubled-edged

left & opposite / performers at the Pic-O-De-Crop competition, part of the Crop Over festival

Bruce Hemming

Bruce Hemming

above & top / Crop Over festival

situation for Barbados, benefiting the nation through exposure and foreign exchange, but threatening to leave a deficit in artistic patrimony.

Partly to correct this, since 1998 the National Art Gallery Committee has been developing a policy and operational system and acquiring works for a national collection. The role of the National Gallery will be not simply to document and preserve the visual arts but to promote and foster a healthy environment for their continued development.

Photography has helped record and interpret Barbados almost since it was invented, leaving a rich legacy of images. Photographs by **Euchard Fitzpatrick**, **Carlton Johnson**, **George Gibbs** and **Edward Stoute** provide evocative records of bygone days. In recent years, fine art photography has been developing at a rapid pace. At least a dozen of the artistic photographers merit mention, but perhaps most visible on this scene are **Ronnie Carrington** and **Bob Kiss**.

There has recently been a tremendous upsurge in efforts to create a local **film industry**, or at least to allow people to tell their own stories, thereby building a cultural identity. Under the auspices of the Faculty of Humanities and Education at UWI, Cave Hill, the **Festival of African and Caribbean Film** initiated educational outreach in the area of film and takes place at more or less regular intervals. **The Film Group** and the **Pan African Commission** also operate in this arena. Each festival includes sessions devoted to technique, meetings with directors, and social gatherings, as well as the screenings themselves. Currently, all three film festivals are beset with financial and organisational challenges.

A handful of Barbadians, most of whom live abroad but who shoot on the island, have produced feature films. **Andrew Millington** and **Miguel Drayton** have each completed a film. At the time of this writing, **Gladstone Yearwood** was in post production, and **Ronnie Carrington**, was in pre-production. Sadly, like filmmakers across the Caribbean, they must contend with marketing and distribution problems.

The local television station, CBC-TV, is now required to show 80 per cent local or Caribbean programming in order to replace the tide of outside images with indigenous ones, and to showcase local talent. This provides an outlet for some local productions.

Festivals & Holidays

The month-long, sugar cane harvest celebration known as **Crop Over** is the highlight of the summer season. With sugar's decline, the crop that is now more celebrated is the year's new calypsos. Based on rhythms that came over from Africa with the slaves, calypso has an infectious beat and clever lyrics that often rely on double entendre. It evolved in two directions. In its social commentary form, it is highly topical, speaking out against corruption, greed and stupidity. In its party form, it is often sexually oriented, and definitely geared for dancing.

Held in November, NIFCA, the **National Independence Festival of Creative Arts**

encompasses the visual, performing, literary and culinary arts. With prizes for professionals and amateurs, adults and children, NIFCA succeeds in stimulating the talents of the whole island. Festival events often reveal these to be considerable.

Organised since 1995 by a government-based secretariat, **Community Independence Celebrations** now take place all over the island. This programme is not merely geared to local cultural and social occasions, but is also developmental, providing parish committees with training sessions in event-planning and public relations skills. Festivities culminate in November with the ceremonial **lighting of Bridgetown** in the national colours and the grand **Spirit of the Nation** pageant and talent showcase.

Barbadians love pageants and hardly a month goes by without one. Pageants have included those that lead to larger competitions, such as **Miss Barbados Universe** as well as thematic ones such as mother-daughter, **Roots Experience**, and **Big and Beautiful**.

Other major festivals include the **Barbados Jazz Festival** and the **Sandy Lane Gold Cup Festival**.

Secular holidays include **New Year's Day**, **Errol Barrow Day** on January 21, **National Heroes Day** on April 28, **Labour Day** on May 1, **Emancipation Day** on August 1, **Kadooment Day** on or around August 7, and **Independence Day** on November 30. Religious holidays are **Good Friday** and **Easter Monday**, **Whit Monday**, **Christmas Day** and **Boxing Day**.

/ Sarah Venable

above & top / performers at the Barbados Jazz Festival

below / children at the Kiddies Kadooment, part of the annual Crop Over festival

Willie Alleyne

Willie Alleyne

above, right, opposite &
following pages / the Grand
Kadooment, Crop Over festival

Willie Alleyne

Willie Alleyne

Willie Alleyne

Willie Alleyne

Bruce Hemming

Cricket: 1966-2006

TRADITIONALLY cricket has been the major sport in Barbados. The game has meant more to the Barbadian public than even soccer to the Brazilians, ice hockey to the Canadians or curling to the Scots. Throughout most of the 20th century, Barbadian politicians, priests and teachers fervently preached the gospel of cricket as they considered the game by far the most effective instrument of social control. Cricket received more tangible and moral support from religious and commercial institutions than any other activity. The result was that Barbados produced more cricket clubs and great cricketers per capita than any other community. By the 1970s, in a country with perhaps fewer than 270,000 souls, there were more than 200 teams operating simultaneously in the Barbados Cricket Association (BCA) and the Barbados Cricket League (BCL).

This unnatural focus on cricket allowed the island to dominate most of the early tournaments in the region and when Barbados achieved political independence in 1966, its leaders thought it appropriate to celebrate the event by challenging the rest of the world to a cricket match at the **Kensington Oval** in Bridgetown. The Rest of the World, which ironically included West Indies stars such as Lance Gibbs and Rohan Kanhai, won that match quite easily. But such was the reputation of this tiny island that many people (both at home and abroad) expressed their utter astonishment that *any* combination of cricketers could possibly prevail against it – especially in its own backyard.

By 1966, Barbados had already produced such world-class players as George Challenor, George Francis, Charlie Griffith, Herman Griffith, Wesley Hall, Conrad Hunte, "Mannie" Martindale, Roy Marshall, Seymour Nurse, Garry Sobers, Clyde Walcott, Everton Weekes and Frank Worrell, among a host of others. The vast

majority of West Indian touring teams had been dominated by the Barbadian contingent. Seven Barbadians, for instance, were in the team of 17 that **Frank Worrell** led to Australia in 1960/61 and John Goddard's squad of 16, who had invaded England so triumphantly in 1950, included as many as six.

This tradition of cricket excellence was continued during the Age of Independence, which coincides exactly with the period of annual first-class competition in the Caribbean archipelago. Amazingly, despite their success at the international level, the West Indies did not manage to establish a regular annual tournament until the inception of the Shell Shield in 1966. Barbados promptly proceeded to win the first two championships, under the direction of the incomparable **Garry Sobers**, who was knighted for his services to the game immediately after his retirement in 1975.

Sobers, in fact, remained the centrepiece of Barbadian cricket for many years. After making his debut against the touring Indians as a slow left-arm spinner in 1953, he blossomed into the greatest all-rounder that the sport has yet spawned. He represented the island on 30 occasions over the next two decades, scoring 2355 runs (at an average of 75.96), capturing 71 wickets (average: 30.04) and holding 22 catches. His batting average is still the highest ever achieved on behalf of Barbados. So long as the mighty Sobers was playing, Barbados remained dominant at home and the West Indies competitive abroad.

Prior to the advent of Sobers, Barbadian and West Indian cricket had revolved around the accomplishments of the **Three Ws** who left an indelible mark throughout the Caribbean. Worrell proved himself the greatest of all West Indian captains, while Walcott in Guyana and Weekes in Barbados did yeoman work coaching the youth. The Three Ws remained excellent role models and many young batsmen, who eventually played for the West Indies, tried to copy their style and method.

The importance that Barbadians have traditionally attached to cricket was revealed amply in the fact that all three members of the famous "W Formation" were elevated to the status of knights, while the Rt Excellent Sir Garfield Sobers was declared a National Hero when that designation was initially created. He is the only living member of the original 10. The Government continues to take advantage of his universal popularity by having him serve as a roving ambassador and a consultant to the Board of Tourism. Recently, too, his expertise has been used by the WICB who appointed him a technical assistant to the coaching team, led by the Australian Bennett King.

After the departure of Sobers, Barbados produced another generation of superstars during the 1970s and 1980s. This crop was led was **Joel Garner**, **Gordon Greenidge**, **Desmond Haynes** and **Malcolm Marshall**, who contributed significantly to the marvellous streak of Caribbean victories during the so-called 'Glory Years' (1975-95). Garner and Marshall were two of the greatest fast bowlers in the history of cricket; Greenidge and Haynes were two of the finest opening batsmen in the world. While Garner and Marshall combined for 635

Graham Morris/AFP/Getty Images

Test wickets at fewer than 21 runs apiece, Greenidge and Haynes between accounted for more than 15,000 Test runs.

In keeping with the Barbadian tendency to glorify their cricketing champions above all others, roundabouts have been named after Sobers and the Three Ws. Pavilions at Kensington have been erected in honour of Challenor, Charlie Griffith & Wes Hall, Greenidge & Haynes, Sobers, and the Three Ws. And bowling ends have been named after Garner and Marshall. Local cricket competitions have also been named after Hunte and Sobers.

Cricket in recent years has lost its absolute supremacy with the emergence of such competing sports as athletics, basketball, field hockey, golf and soccer, but it still remains relatively supreme in the sense that it has more adherents than any other single rival. This development is reflected in the composition of recent West Indian squads. Whereas the Barbadians once accounted for almost half of the touring teams, they are now in a distinct minority.

Their finest cricketers in recent years have been Tino Best, Ian Bradshaw, Courtney Browne, Corey Collymore, Pedro Collins, Fidel Edwards, Ryan Hinds and Dwayne Smith. But none of them has yet achieved superstar status. Even so, Barbados has continued to dominate the regional competition winning no fewer than 19 of the first 40 titles. This is best put into perspective when considering that Jamaica, far larger and more populous, has won only six times in that span. Most worrisome is the noticeable decline in Barbadian batsmanship. The community has not produced a world-class middle-order batsman since the departure of Seymour Nurse in 1969. Perhaps the chief culprits here are the groundsmen, who have persisted since the 1970s in preparing green and bouncy strips to favour the faster bowlers. The BCA would do well to monitor wicket preparation more aggressively, to ensure that the pitches offer both bat and ball an equal chance.

above / former West Indies batsman Gordon Greenidge (centre), who formed one of the great opening pairings in Test cricket with fellow Barbadian Desmond Haynes, talks to members of the Bangladesh national side, which he coached to the ICC Trophy victory that helped ensure the country was granted Test status from November 2000

Barbados-born cricketers who have represented West Indies at Test level

PLAYER	TESTS	Runs	Average	Wickets	Average		WK Ct	WK St
David Walter Allan	5	75	12.50			Wicket Keeper	15	3
Dennis St Eval Atkinson †	22	922	31.79	47	35.04			
Eric St Eval Atkinson	8	126	15.75	25	23.56			
Edward Lawson Bartlett	5	131	18.71					
Carlisle Alonza Best	8	342	28.50					
Tino la Bertram Best *	12	174	10.23	26	45.03			
Lionel Sidney Birkett	4	136	17.00	1	71.00			
Keith David Boyce	21	657	24.33	60	30.01			
Ian David Russell Bradshaw *	5	96	13.71	9	60.00			
Courtney Oswald Browne	20	387	16.12			Wicket Keeper	79	2
Cyril Rutherford Browne	4	176	25.14	6	48.00			
Michael Robin Bynoe	4	111	18.50	1	5.00			
Sherwin Legay Campbell	52	2882	32.38					
George McDonald Carew	4	170	28.33					
George Challenor	3	101	16.83					
Carlos Bertram Clarke	3	3	1.00	6	43.50			
Sylvester Theophilus Clarke	11	172	15.63	42	27.85			
Pedro Tyrone Collins *	32	235	5.87	106	34.63			
Corey Delano Collymore *	23	149	7.84	75	29.58			
Anderson Cleophas Cummins	5	98	19.60	8	42.75			
Wayne Wendell Daniel	10	46	6.57	36	25.27			
Cyril Clairmonte De Peiaza	5	187	31.16					
Vasbert Conniel Drakes	12	386	21.44	33	41.27			
Fidel Henderson Edwards *	24	119	4.25	62	43.14			
Richard Martin Edwards	5	65	9.28	18	34.77			
George Nathaniel Francis	10	81	5.78	23	33.17			
Michael Campbell Frederick	1	30	15.00					
Joel Garner	58	672	12.44	259	20.97			
Ottis Delroy Gibson	2	93	23.25	3	91.66			
John Douglas Claude Goddard †	27	859	30.67	33	31.81			
Alvin Ethelbert Greenidge	6	222	22.20					
Cuthbert Gordon Greenidge †	108	7558	44.72					
Geoffrey Alan Greenidge	5	209	29.85					
Adrian Frank Gordon Griffith	14	638	24.53					
Charles Christopher Griffith	28	530	16.56	94	28.54			
Herman Clarence Griffith	18	91	5.05	44	28.25	Born in Trinidad 1893		
Wesley Winfield Hall	48	818	15.73	192	26.38			
Desmond Leo Haynes †	116	7487	42.49	1	8.00			
Ryan O'Neal Hinds *	9	363	24.20	5	78.00			
Edward Lisle Goldsworthy Hoad †	4	98	12.25					

Continued ...

The BCA, however, is limited in what it can attempt to do. It is severely hamstrung by the lack of funds. For one glorious stretch, during 1978-90, it profited enormously from the success of the Instant Money Game (IMG) that Peter Lashley, a former player and one of its vice-presidents, had introduced and masterminded. The returns from that experiment permitted the BCA to renovate the old Kensington Oval and add a significant number of new stands and pavilions. It was also able to offer attractive prizes to clubs and players for excellent performances. But the IMG steadily faded during the 1990s when faced with serious competition from other national lotteries. This has left the BCA at the mercy of its members, clubs and sponsors.

The number of BCA members increased rapidly during the early years of Independence. In 1947, the roll stood at 99. The Association was then little more than a white man's club, dominated by a few families (representing mainly two clubs, Pickwick and Wanderers). The numbers mushroomed in the 1960s, reaching 609 by 1970. During the 1970s the spiral continued, reaching 858 by 1979. By the end of the 20th century the BCA boasted in excess of 1,750 members.

There was also a notable increase in the number of clubs claiming BCA affiliation. In 1950, there were only 17 BCA clubs. This number rose steadily to 50 in 1985 and to 80 by the end of the century. Even if a number of the clubs recently seeking entry into the BCA had formerly been members of the BCL, these impressive statistics debunk the myth that cricket has lost its hold on the Barbadian populace.

The BCA, established as a successor to the Challenge Cup Committee in 1933, did not seek any sponsorship during its early years. The aggressive quest for sponsors came only after the introduction of the Shell Shield and then intensified after the Packer Revolution in the late 1970s. Kerry Packer, the wealthy Australian television magnate, had shown the whole cricket world what sponsors and sponsorships could accomplish for the sport as well as individual businesses.

Hence the establishment of the Marketing Committee that has become one of the most important arms of the BCA. Such sponsors as the Barbados American Tobacco Company (BAT), the Barbados Fire & General Insurance Company (later BF&C), Benson & Hedges, A S Bryden & Sons Ltd, Bubba's, Cable & Wireless Ltd (now BET), the Canadian Imperial Bank of Commerce (CIBC), Cave Shepherd & Co Ltd, Court's, Goddard Enterprises Ltd, Hanschell Inniss Ltd, Jason Jones, Neal & Massy, Northern Telecom, Suzuki and Yellow Pages have made useful contributions. From these sources the BCA in recent years has received close to $250,000 annually. Given the dramatic increase in the costs of the game at all levels, however, a great deal more is still needed.

On the field, the older clubs (Empire, Pickwick, Spartan and Wanderers) dominated the First Division competition for many years. In recent times, however, some of the younger clubs – such as Banks, Maples and St Catherine – have begun to challenge them very seriously.

above / boundaries and bouncers have always been what cricket-crazy Barbadians like to see most, as the island has produced an amazing array of glorious, strokemaking batsmen and brilliant fast bowlers

PLAYER	MATCHES	Runs	Average	Wickets	Average		WKCt	WKSt
Roland Irwin Christopher Holder	11	380	25.33					
Vanburn Alonzo Holder	40	682	14.20	109	33.27			
David Anthony Jerome Holford	24	768	22.58	51	39.37			
Anthony Bourne Howard	1	D	2.00	70				
Conrad Cleophas Hunte	44	3245	45.06	2	55			
Collis Llewellyn King	9	418	32.15	3	94			
Frank McDonald King	14	116	8.28	29	39.96			
Patrick Douglas Lashley	4	159	22.71	1	1.00			
Malcolm Denzil Marshall	81	1810	18.45	376	20.94			
Norman Edgar Marshall	1	8	4.00	2	31.00			
Roy Edwin Marshall	4	143	20.42					
Emanuel Alfred Martindale	10	58	5.27	37	21.72			
Ezra Alphonsa Moseley	2	35	8.75	6	43.5			
David Anthony Murray	19	601	21.46			Wicket Keeper	57	5
James Montague Neblett	1	16	16.00	1	75			
Seymour McDonald Nurse	29	2523	47.6					
Albert Leroy Padmore	2	8	8.00	1	135.00			
Thelston Rodney O'Neale Payne	1	5	5.00					
Floyd Lamonte Reifer	4	63	7.87					
James Edward Derrick Sealy	11	478	28.11	3	31.33			
John Neil Shepherd	5	77	9.62	19	25.21			
Milton Aster Small	2	3	-	4	38.25			
Cameron Wilberforce Smith	5	222	24.66					
Dwayne Romel Smith	10	320	24.61	7	49.14			
Garfield St Auburn Sobers [†]	93	8032	57.78	235	34.03			
Patterson Ian Thompson	2	17	8.50	5	43.00			
Clyde Leopold Walcott	44	3798	56.68	11	37.09			
Leslie Arthur Walcott	1	40	40	1	32.00			
Philo Alphonso Wallace	7	279	21.46					
Everton de Courcy Weekes	48	4455	58.61	1	77.00			
Anthony Wilbur White	2	71	23.66	3	50.66			
Charles Archibald Wiles	1	2	1.00					
Ernest Albert Vivian Williams	4	113	18.83	9	26.77			
Frank Mortimer Maglinne Worrell [†]	51	3860	49.48	69	38.72			

Barbados-born players who played Test cricket for England

Roland Orlando Butcher	3	71	14.20		
Gladstone Cleophas Small	17	263	15.47	55	34.01

* Current player – statistics correct to October 1, 2006.   *† Captain of West Indies*

NB Courtney Browne (London) and Herman Griffith (Trinidad) were born outside Barbados, but played their first-class cricket for the island

Of the major developments that have taken place in Barbadian cricket during the Age of Independence, the most obvious is the decline of the white element as players and administrators. Prior to the 1960s, the BCA Board of Management was composed mainly of white and wealthy males. Such clubs as Pickwick, Leeward, Wanderers and Windward represented the planter class. Carlton and YMPC catered to the middle-income Whites and Mulattoes. Spartan spoke for the middle-class Blacks and Empire for the lower-middle income Blacks. The BCL had been established deliberately in 1937 to give poor Blacks, especially in the rural areas, their only available form of organized cricket.

These socio-economic barriers have all been removed. Blacks dominate Barbadian cricket at all levels and the lily-white clubs have been legislated out of existence. With the dramatic explosion of the Barbadian bourgeoisie since the 1960s, the traditional boundaries – even those between the BCA and the BCL – have become increasingly blurred.

These, by and large, are positive signs as they reflect the gradual democratisation of the sport. But older pundits are left to regret the demotion of the secondary schools from the BCA First Division competition. After all, such schools as Combermere, Harrison College and the Lodge had served as the most effective cricket nurseries for at least 100 years prior to the Age of Independence.

Also regrettable is the fact that the pupils of secondary schools are encouraged to take part in limited-overs cricket before having fully acquired the basic skills necessary for successful participation in the longer versions of the game. This is reflected especially in the general weakness of Barbadian (and West Indian) batting for an unconscionably long time.

If West Indian cricket has languished in the past dozen years, this is due largely to the fact that the quality of play in Barbados has also deteriorated. There is a sound basis for the old adage that West Indian cricket prospers when Barbadian cricket is powerful. Barbadians, therefore, must seek to return to their old lofty heights for the sake of the region.

The whole society must become involved in this cricket renaissance. Schools have to make cricket a more regular feature of physical education programmes. Commercial houses have to be more generous in their support of the game. The Government must also seek, by whatever means, to promote the sport as a symbol of national excellence. The BCA and the BCL must redouble their efforts to encourage former stars to coach and mentor the young. And the community must publish, collect and disseminate cricket videos and books that can serve a dual purpose; they teach the youth how to play the game and they inspire the general public to learn more about (and to preserve) the rich legacy that is Barbadian and Caribbean cricket.

/ Keith Sandiford

above / cricket, lovely cricket – the sport is integral to the Barbados way of life, from local club matches and inter-island contests to the hosting of Test matches, which attract a vast number of sports tourists, especially when England are in town

Other Bajan Sports Stars

Cricket legends notwithstanding, Barbados has produced several outstanding individuals that have left an indelible mark on the regional and international sporting landscape.

IT IS OFTEN said that after cricket in Barbados, the discipline of **bodybuilding** has given the world an outstanding set of sporting heroes, who have not only competed well but have also gone to the top rung of the sport.

When you talk about **Earl Maynard** you refer to a giant that won three *Mr Universe* titles and one *Mr World*. He was recognised duly internationally in 2002, when he was inducted into the *British Sports and Fitness Hall of Fame*. He was in fine company, too, as the famous Arnold Schwarzenegger was also inducted on the same night. We might add that Maynard has also appeared in 17 Hollywood movies and only recently wrote, produced and directed his own film, *Flight of The Mongoose*, as well as producing a documentary on Barbados entitled *Enchanting Barbados*.

Maynard gets the most notice with his credentials but there are others like Darcy Beckles who won *Mr World*, Roy Callender (*Mr Universe*) and Bernard Sealy (*Mr World short class*). Not far behind are champions in their own right like Patrick Nicholls, Loftus Roach, Roger Boyce and others of more recent vintage including Lynden Belgrave and Carmichael Bryan, who are now campaigning as professionals. It should be noted that we have not been selfish in keeping this magnitude of talent here in our midst as Barbados-born Albert Beckles, competing for Britain, also won the *Mr Universe* crown. Astonishingly, Beckles at 80 is still a personal trainer!

A few women have also carved out a notable mark in the bodybuilding discipline. They include Maggie Callender, the queen of them all, Jenny Beckles and Angela Sealy. They dominated at regional level while in their prime. A few pretenders have tried to walk in their footsteps but they have not been able to sustain their interest in what is a very demanding sport in terms of commitment and the sacrifices that have to be made.

Very high on the list of individual performances in the past 40 years will have to be sports ambassador **Obadele Thompson,** who lifted the spirit of the nation in 2000 at the Sydney Olympics, where he won a bronze medal in the blue riband event of any major games – the **100 metres**. It was this country's first individual medal at the Olympics, though **Jim Wedderburn** also won a bronze medal as part of the West Indies **4 x 400 metres relay** squad at the 1960 Rome Olympics. Those were the days when the Caribbean flirted briefly with a federation. Some of Thompson's other outstanding feats include the fact that he is among a handful of sprinters who were able to win the sprint double at the testing NCAA championships in the United States. He did so in 1996. He also ran the fastest time ever recorded under any conditions, a blistering 9.69 seconds in 1995, but unfortunately it was not recognised as a world record because it was adjudged to have been wind-assisted.

It has to be stated that the foundation for Oba's success would have been laid by several other shining stars, who may not have had the same level of exposure as he did leading up to a major undertaking like the Olympics. We are always reminded of Orlando 'Snoops' Greene, who had the leading time in the world in the **800 metres** before the 1976 Montreal Olympics, but because he was under-prepared he was not able to live up to expectations. It must not be forgotten that the men's **4 x 400 metres relay** team of Richard Louis, Elvis Forde, David Peltier and Clyde Edwards reached the final of the Los Angeles Olympics in 1984. High jumper Anton Norris was also a standout in his event, having a Commonwealth silver medal among others to show for his immense ability. It has not been only about the men. The late Patsy Callender was as good an all-round athlete as any but there again she may not have had the degree of exposure or experience to take her to the next level. A stand at the National Stadium has been named after her. Few will dispute that Barbados had an outstanding quartet of excellent female **sprinting** jewels in the form of Marcia Trotman, Freida Nicholls, Lorna Forde and Yolande Straughn, all of whom represented their country at the Olympics. In recent years diminutive **400-metre hurdler**, Andrea Blackett, has served her country well in her event, finishing 2005 as the sixth-ranked athlete in the world in this category.

Great strides have been made in **track and field** but it must be noted that some

above / athletic pursuits – men and women sprinters in Barbados dream of Olympic glory

overleaf / Obadele Thompson (right) carries the Barbados flag after taking the bronze medal in the Men's 100m Final at the 2000 Olympic Games in Sydney, Australia. Alongside him are gold medallist, Maurice Greene of the USA (centre) and silver medallist, Ato Boldon of Trinidad and Tobago

Mike Powell /Allsport

above / sport is in the blood of most Barbadians, who love to take part in a wide variety of sports from football and netball to road tennis, which was invented on the island, and could one day go global

of those who have excelled have done so as a result of gaining scholarships to American Universities, where they were afforded the opportunity to compete against some of the best among their peers in the world, while giving them the chance to also further their education. This movement was started by the late Louis Lynch, a true pioneer in promoting the concept of education and sports as disciplines you can do together and be successful doing both. Since his passing this role has been taken up by noted club coaches like Jerston Clarke and Anthony Lovell as well as others like Ron Boyce and Elvis Forde, who have strong links with American institutions as coaches. Generally, there are great technical resources at home to provide the foundation for further success once they go overseas. Former top sprinter Frank Blackman, for instance, has become even more revered for his involvement with Obadele Thompson's success.

It is arguable if Barbados has produced a more charismatic champion than **checkers** genius Ronald 'Suki' King. King has been world champion in the 'go-as-you-please' form for the past 14 years. Fittingly, King's alma mater, Workman's Primary erected a bust of him at the entrance of the school. He has also been credited with bringing what was considered a backstreet sport to the fore in Barbados. His rival Jack Francis has done extremely well against his international peers in the past decade as well.

As far as team sports are concerned not even cricket has been as successful on a sustained basis as **volleyball** at the regional level. The men's team completed its 10th successive Caribbean title. They have competed in 11 overall, meaning that they lost only the very first time that they competed. The women's team has also prospered, though has yet to match the success of their male counterparts.

As an indigenous discipline, Barbados has given **Road Tennis** to the world. The world body is based on the island and it is felt that once there is a more effect drive to market it universally the sport could very well take the world by storm. The sport would have had its working-class origins in areas like Lakes Folly, New Orleans, Bush Hall and Deacons. The late Lance Bynoe was one of the central figures, who staged organised tournaments in the 1950s. A typical Road Tennis court measures 22ft x 10ft, with a centre piece measuring 10ft wide x 8 inches high. It is played with a wooden racquet and a skinned tennis ball. The sport has naturally provided its stars like Deighton 'Pa' Roach, who has a community venue in Bush Hall named after him, Keith Griffith, Ormond Hoyte, Anthony 'Limp' Richardson, Antonio Daniel, Curtis 'Socks' Bailey and Sandra Bailey.

In the area of **horseracing** there have been many riders who, given the chance, could hold their own against the best in the world. Eric Holder, Johnny Belle, Smirkey Blades, Byron Clarke, Challenor Jones, Venice Richards and now Patrick Husbands, who campaigns on the North American circuit with a base at Woodbine in Toronto, Canada, are some of the best known. There are household names among the animals, too, including the horse regarded as the best to have come to these shores in *Mentone. Fairy Valley, Blue Print, Bentom, Stangrave Park, Incatatus, Kingly Street* and *Stanford Prince* to name but a few.

There have been other outstanding talents in other sports including **footballers**

Victor 'Gas' Clarke, the late Reggie Haynes, a member of the West Indies team to England in 1959, Carlos 'Chuckberry' Griffith, who died in the floods of 1970, Harcourt 'Pow' Hinds, Eric Alleyne, Anthony 'Daisley' Clarke, Jerry Goddard and Adrian Hall. **Netball's** biggest name is centre Marva Harris Sealy but through the years there have also been others like June Carew Benjamin, Maureen Weithers, the Banfield sisters – Sonja and Sonia – Lorna Rouse, Carolyn Sinckler, Jackie Forde and Margaret Greaves. Debra Lynch and Marion Johnson Hurley were also outstanding national players, who have also made their mark as international umpires.

The one name Barbados will always associate with **swimming** is Leah Martindale, who became the first black woman to reach an Olympic final, coming fourth in the 50 metres at the 1996 Atlanta Olympics. Chris Gibbs was outstanding as both a swimmer and a water polo player. He will be remembered best for being the only Caribbean swimmer to swim the English Channel, which he did in 2004. His brother, Peter Gibbs, also made history by swimming Lake Ontario, Canada, a year later. Also the names of Phil Als and Randall Valdez will not be forgotten anytime soon, as they became the first people from the region to row across the Atlantic in 2003.

Cycling's icons began with Ken Farnum in the 1950s and progressed to the 1970s when Kensley Reece and Hector Edwards were dominant. The next shining light was Barry Forde, who has also been the most decorated but also the most controversial, having had his problems with the drug authorities.

above / Barbadians have made their mark on a broader stage in swimming, cycling and boxing

Few appear to know that Joe Walcott, who was born in Saint Joseph, was a **world boxing champion** in the welterweight division in the late 19th century. Tyrone Downes, a featherweight, became a Commonwealth Champion in the early 1980s. Christopher 'Shaka' Henry also became a world champion in 2004, under the International Boxing Union. Other boxing stars included Young Badou, Young Cassius Clay, Edwin Pollard and Edward 'Yogi Bear' Neblett, who once trained and sparred with the legendary Sugar Ray Leonard. Eric Sealy stands out as the top promoter.

The **weightlifter** most talked about is Anthony 'Mango' Philips, who took his craft and skill to major games and medalled.

Some of the revered **administrators** include Austin Sealy in athletics and the Olympic movement, Esther Maynard in the same field, Captain Peter Short and the late Mitchie Hewitt in cricket, the late Christie Smith in football, the late Honor Skinner in Tennis, Keith Morris in table tennis, Kathy Harper-Hall in a number of other sports but netball, in particular, and Steve Stoute, originally in cycling but now the Olympic movement too.

All in all Barbados can boast of being a very small nation that has given the sporting world some very big giants.

/ Andi Thornhill

Tourism – A Centuries-old Tradition

opposite top / Lone Star opened in 1997 immediately bringing a new dimension to the restaurant scene in Barbados. With polished wooden floors, mahogany framed mirrors, and a cool blue and white decor, the minimalist design is immediately apparent. Once combined in a spectacular ocean front location with wonderful beach views, the result is simply magnificent. Converted from the old coralstone 'Lone Star Garage' built in the 1940s, Christian Roberts, the English owner and former actor, really has created something special. The truly international menu ranges from Indian Balti dishes to tempura shrimp and grilled fresh lobster. Managed discreetly by Rory Rodger since 1998, the restaurant has gone from strength to strength over the years and now attracts world leaders, international sports stars and 'A-list' celebrities from Hollywood and London

opposite bottom / The Bridgetown Cruise Terminal provides convenient access to shops and other facilities to cruise passengers in a spacious and colourful atmosphere. The Bridgetown Cruise Terminal is the centre for all services provided for the use of cruise passengers and crewmembers visiting Barbados. It offers more than 60,000 square feet of space, with some 20,000 sq ft allocated to shops and the remainder space for the offices of Customs, Immigration, Port Health, Plant and Animal Quarantine, Post Office and the Barbados Tourism Authority. In addition to the diverse shopping experience available, the terminal also operates a fully air-conditioned, state-of-the-art Telecommunications Centre that allows users to reach anywhere in the world by telephone, fax or email. Multi-lingual hostesses are on hand to ensure that visitors receive any necessary assistance in placing their calls

TOURISM in Barbados has a long and distinguished history. As early as the 18th century the island was noted for its health tourism. Nineteen-year-old **George Washington** spent his only days outside the continental USA at the side of his ailing brother, Lawrence, who was sent to recover his health in Barbados away from the harsh northern winter of 1751.

The British West Indies forces in the Caribbean also provided important revenue to the 18th-century economy – perhaps the purists will dispute this as a proper element of tourism – but the British forces were visitors, they brought money into the economy and they required paid services, of all kinds, from locals.

The **19th century** continued from the previous era with the heavy involvement of the military, as many of the upper class Navy officers (including a future King of England) used Barbados to rest and recreate during lulls in their service throughout the Caribbean and Atlantic regions. That period (1750-1850) saw the proliferation of **Town Hotels** owned by mulatto women, many of whom were based on or near the main street of the city. Of course, there were also suburban and countryside hotels such as **Seaview**, the **Crane** and **Bathsheba** on the East Coast.

Since the **Second World War**, however, Barbados has experienced its most important phase of what is now seen as 'sun, sand and sea' tourism. Dozens of Officers from the British Services found their way to Barbados to recover from the trauma of the Theatres of War; many of them stayed, mostly to build or buy homes far away from the cold winters of England.

Several of these homes, especially on the **St James coast**, were soon turned into clubs, the forerunners of hotels such as **Coral Reef**, **Colony**, **Miramar** and later

above & right / South Beach Resort and Vacation Club is located in the heart of the island's lively south coast, directly opposite the glistening white sands and crystal waters of Rockley Beach. South Beach has a total of 49 rooms distributed over five floors. Designed to make residents feel at home, their large suites are all fitted with kitchenettes or kitchens and have the added attraction of having a Jacuzzi in each room. Also in the group is the Sea Breeze Beach Hotel, consisting of 31 studio apartments, 45 rooms and two two-bedroom apartments. With its unrivalled beachfront location, the rooms are spread over almost three acres of beautifully landscaped grounds in several three-storey buildings. Their food and beverage facilities consist of three restaurants and bars: Fish Pot Beach and Pool Bar, The Pavilion Restaurant and the elegant Mermaid Restaurant. Finally, there is Ocean One, located on half a mile of beach at Maxwell Coast Road, also on the south coast. It is conveniently situated with easy access to an abundance of restaurants, bars, banks and stores, while the airport and the highway are also minutes away. There are just 21 residences spread over six levels, ensuring privacy and intimacy in two and three bedroom penthouse suites.

Royal Pavilion, **Glitter Bay** and **Cobblers Cove**. Later, there were also transfers from sugar to sand, as in the case of **Sam Lord's Castle**, **Rockley**, **Sandy Lane**, **Heywood's**, **Durant's** and the **Royal Westmoreland** golf establishments, which were located on former sugar lands or infrastructure.

There were also some upper-crust officers of the **British and Canadian Forces**, who came to the island just before or immediately after **D-Day**. This group included **Carlyon Bellairs**, who later bequeathed his St James residence, becoming the Bellairs Research Institute of the McGill's University. **Murtogh Guinness** was a regular visitor, who lived on this coast from 1942.

Ronald Tree, equerry to Sir Winston Churchill, built a Palladian mansion on a nearby heron swamp and soon invited Royalty from both sides of the Atlantic to visit. His impressive guest list included **Her Majesty and Prince Philip**, **Princesses Margaret** and **Alexandra** and their consorts at several and different times, British Prime Ministers **Sir Winston Churchill** and **Sir Anthony Eden**, as well as Canadian PM **John Diefenbaker**. **President Clinton**, the **Rockefellers** and **Hubert Humphrey** were able representatives of the USA to write their names in the Guest Book at 'Heron Beach'. **Ronald Reagan** also lived on the west coast in 1982 when he visited long-time resident **Claudette Colbert**, the Academy Award-winning actress.

It is not difficult to see that with some specific marketing, these iconic figures would be followed by numbers of their compatriots, if only to see where their idols had visited. Many British and American visitors have remarked that they were able to see their leaders in Barbados for the first time in person.

The Barbados Tourism Authority is the successor-marketing agency to the various Committees and Boards, whose task since the 1940s has been to capitalize mainly on the associations that developed between Barbados and its influential visitors. The rather independent outlook of a small island, whose nickname is 'little England', has also helped, especially in encouraging British visitors, the current leading source of revenue to the Barbados economy.

Canadian Prime Minister **Pierre Trudeau** was also a guest in the sixties. His visit preceded the development of Sunset Crest, a holiday village also located on the Saint James coast. There is no coincidence that early ownership of these holiday bungalows rested almost entirely with Canadians so that Barbados has experienced a good mix of visitor arrivals from both sides of the Atlantic, even though the United Kingdom now provides the major portion of arrivals.

Projections and Prospects

Since 1980 a conscious effort has been made to construct a tourism component based upon sports. Major attractions including field hockey, horse racing, road-running events, and of course cricket, have been the magnet for a new wave of young and not so young visitors, who come mainly to participate in, or spectate at, sporting events that are listed on the tourism calendar of events.

top & above / a little gem and a surprisingly well-kept secret, Treasure Beach offers a stunning location, quiet, intimate charm and service with a smile. Located on one of the island's best white sand beaches, the 35-room hotel is set in lush, tropical gardens. Newly modernised, the hotel also offers new luxury suites with private pools overlooking the Caribbean Sea. The 'Al Fresco' restaurant is a must, where delicious cooking, using fresh local ingredients, combines with dining under the stars

The mid-year carnival, known locally as 'Crop Over', also contributes heavily to visitor arrivals, mainly from the Caribbean and North America. Most recently world-class golf events and now the **World Cup of Cricket** are seen as superlative events that will drive a new legacy of competence in Barbados to organize and execute events at the highest level.

The prospects for the immediate future look good and an annual increase of two per cent in long-stay arrivals is expected to constitute the mainstay of national revenues over the next five years.

/ Morris Greenidge

above and opposite / Elegant Hotels live up to their name, with five distinctly different hotels on the island from which to choose. On the sun-kissed shoreline, where tropical beaches meet sparkling Caribbean seas, your enchanting stay in Barbados becomes complete as their cordial staff welcome travellers to their own private oasis

left top / with its beautiful oceanfront setting and lush indoor gardens, Pisces has long been one of the island's more sought after spots to dine. Pisces offers visitors an international menu with a subtle West Indian influence and features an extensive variety of fresh seafood. This seaside restaurant with its friendly service and comfortable yet charming ambience should not be missed

left bottom / Daphne's Restaurant offers an idyllic setting for al fresco dining on this pristine West coast beach, with its cooling balmy trade winds and spectacular sunsets. The unique talents of chef Marco Festini and traditional hospitality of manager Marco Pavone combine to provide a feast of elegant modern Italian dining. Daphne's stands as an integral part of the Elegant Hotels Group

top, above & right / comprising three prime beachfront properties all situated on the south coast of Barbados, this group of hotels comprises the Amaryllis Beach Resort, which is set on 5.5 acres with 150 rooms, the Sandy Bay Beach Club, an all-inclusive property nestled in a lush tropical setting, and the Allamanda Beach Hotel, which has 50 self-contained rooms

opposite top / come experience the warmth and comfort that Barbados is renowned for, with over 40 unique properties that make up the Intimate Hotels of Barbados. Their serene seaside villas, charming apartment hotels and cosy guesthouses are located on the picturesque west and south coasts of the island, ensuring guests are always within reach of Barbados' finest restaurants, beaches, shopping and nightlife

opposite bottom / the Barbados Beach Club makes the most of the natural facilities – warm Caribbean sunshine, an incredible blue sky, soft white sand, coconut palms swaying in cooling trade winds and a dazzling aquamarine sea – and combines them with the best man-made offerings. Enjoy delicious well-prepared meals, varied entertainment, interesting drinks, a round of tennis or mini-golf, a refreshing swim in the pool or sample water sports in an all-inclusive package

above / Reefers & Wreckers is a family-run dive shop situated in historic Speightstown. They offer tailored dive packages to suite all levels of experience on the unspoilt reefs and ever-evolving wrecks off the Barbadian coastline. All their instructors and dive masters are PADI certified experts with first-class reputations for their friendly, personalised service

left / the Cobblers Cove Hotel, Saint Peter. Their objective is simple; they want every guest that stays at the hotel to return and hope that they tell their friends and family about them

opposite top / the Skyviews team in Barbados, with office mascots! For over 20 years this family-owned and operated business has been creating visitor guides to the Caribbean islands. These high quality, high definition glossy pocket maps, endorsed by the Tourist Boards on various islands, depict topographical, commercial and cultural information intended to introduce visitors to products, services and sights on the island. Cyberspace visitors can also look at the extensive interactive website to learn more about the islands. Skyviews is a major player in the development and viability of promoting the variety of services and range of activities available on each of these unique Caribbean territories. After 20 years in the market of creating and building corporate identities, a second company, Skyviews Caribbean Ltd, was established through the need to provide clients with an auxiliary range of services and products

opposite bottom/ Atlantis Submarines remains a unique and spectacular way to experience underwater Barbados. Guests sit in air-conditioned comfort and safety, descending to 150 feet while enjoying the humorous tales of the co-pilot and pilot. Once below water colourful fish play and graceful turtles glide by. They seem to be as curious about the submarine as its passengers are of them. Atlantis Submarine is Zagat rated and is winner of the inaugural Tourism Award of Excellence for attractions

Willie Alleyne

above / the Divi Southwinds Beach Resort is located along the south coast of Barbados, with a unique location on the lively St Lawrence Gap that offers easy access to first-class restaurants and nightlife. The resort features spacious one and two bedroom suites with fully equipped kitchens and private balconies with pool, ocean, and garden views. Amenities include three swimming pools, two restaurants, fitness centre, tennis, and mini-market

left / the Lucky Horseshoe has a unique, American-influenced menu that offers breakfast, lunch and dinner around the clock. There's a sizeable bar, large-screen televisions showing the latest in sports or music via satellite and slot machines for adults. Families are well catered for with the Super Value Kids Menu or the Kids Eat Free specials. The Lucky Horseshoe is now at two locations, Warrens and Worthing

above / the brand new Hilton Barbados has all the amenities you could want, boasting two white-sand beaches, sprawling swimming pools, water activity centre, spa treatment rooms, Kidz Paradise Club, three tennis courts and a fitness centre. All 350 rooms feature spectacular ocean views, private balconies, separate bathtub and shower, high-speed internet access and all Hilton amenities to make you feel at home

right / since its opening, Bubba's has become the ideal spot for lunch or dinner, and a prime location for viewing all sporting events via satellite. In fact, no other facility can compare to Bubba's three 10ft screens and 12 plasma televisions that allow patrons to watch live English Premiership football, NFL football, NBA basketball, Formula One motor racing, tennis and hockey. This ultra-modern facility offers an array of scrumptious appetisers on their extensive menu

above / the Restaurant at Southsea, St Lawrence Gap, Christ Church, has been named the BHTA Restaurant of the Year two years running and is the only restaurant in Barbados to be given a Four Diamond rating by the Triple A Association. Picked by the celebrated Conde Nast Traveller Hot List during its first year of operation, the restaurant boasts stunning ocean views and amiable service. Chef Barry Taylor creates epicurean ecstasy, back by exceptional wine list and the Caribbean's most extensive vintage rum collection

left / Josef's Restaurant offers classical international and seafood cuisine complemented with its new contemporary, air-conditioned Japanese Restaurant upstairs. Josef's is set in a beautifully restored Barbadian home, amongst lush gardens and dining gazebos, situated on a cliff with breathtaking views of the Caribbean. It is a magnificent venue for large gatherings and weddings, as well as intimate dinners for two

Getting Married in Barbados

BARBADOS has proved itself to be the island of choice for romantics from all over the world as they hunt the globe for the perfect location for one of the biggest celebrations of their lives – their destination wedding!

So just why do these ever-increasing numbers of visitors elect to tie the knot on the tiny island of Barbados? Because they dream, and dream big, and Barbados fulfils their dreams for romance, intimacy and natural beauty! Coupled with this is the fact that the weather is as consistently perfect as weather can be. Technically it is located outside the official hurricane belt, which is another plus factor – it just does not get any better than this!

Weddings...beyond Your Imagination!!

Couples...

Imagine... saying "I do", with the one you love under brilliant blue Barbadian skies, as the sun kisses your cheeks and the Trade Winds play with your hair!!

Imagine... a tropical seashore garden, or... sand between your toes, as crystal clear waves gently lap the shore, and palm trees sway overhead, as the sweet sounds of a live steel band serenade you in paradise!!

Imagine... the convenience of combining the wedding and honeymoon of your dreams 'in paradise', surrounded by your closest loved ones, while avoiding the large formal affairs often expected by extended family and friends back home.

Whatever the motivation, there is certainly no shortage of excited couples happy to tie the knot in Barbados, nor facilities and service providers to accommodate their every desire no matter how simple, elaborate or creative they aspire to be. Venues and entertainment options for their ceremony, reception, rehearsal dinner, welcome cocktail parties and farewell brunches are almost endless and may be hosted onshore or under sail

as desired. Over the years visitors have become 'one' in **churches**, **hotels**, **restaurants**, **historical sites**, **private homes**, **holiday villas** and **gardens**, not to mention the more adventurous, who have married **barefoot on the beach**; down under in **Harrison's Cave**, underwater aboard the **Atlantis Submarine** or in full scuba gear; in the shadow of an authentic **Lighthouse**, under sail bikini-style aboard **coastal cruisers** or in full regalia in the middle of **Kensington Oval**, where the World Cup Cricket Final is scheduled to be played in 2007.

Statically, non-national nuptials have been booming with Visitor weddings on the island exceeding local ones since 1973, many of British origin with Barbados being voted their No1 destination for weddings and honeymoons.

Barbados continues to be a destination of choice for many and its popularity has grown as a preferred destination for visitor weddings since being chosen for the *Bride's Magazine /Air Jamaica* 'Love is in the air' promotion culminating in a wedding of a lifetime on the island in October 1999. After years of being in the limelight, **Liv Tyler** and **Royston Langdon**

above & left / Barbados has become a popular wedding destination that can cater for those wanting anything from a beachside ceremony to a large traditional church service. Barbados-based wedding organiser *Weddings...beyond Your Imagination!!* work to provide couples with the wedding of their dreams. Blue skies, swaying trees and golden beaches, gently lapped by a crystal-clear sea, provides the wedding backdrop... and then, step straight into the honeymoon!

flew to a private villa to exchange their vows in a romantic affair in March 2003. International media exposure of Barbados as a preferred destination wedding location again followed after the extravagant wedding of world champion golfer, **Tiger Woods** and **Elin Nordegren** in October 2004, and in July 2005 when **Jemma Kidd** married 28-year-old **Arthur Wellesley**, the Earl of Mornington, who will eventually become the Duke of Wellington.

This irresistible urge to merge in Barbados has been encouraged by Government with the legal requirements for Marriage being simplified completely. There is no required waiting period, or minimum length of stay – couples may marry immediately following the procuring of a Marriage Licence from the Ministry of Home Affairs, thus facilitating a similar growth in the number of weddings by cruise ship passengers. Couples are welcome to sail into port as lovers and sail off into the sunset as husband and wife that very same afternoon!

The Bride and Groom must apply for their Marriage Licence together and in person at the Ministry of Home Affairs, with the following documentation in hand:

- Valid Passports or the original or certified copies of Birth Certificates.

- If either party was divorced, an original Decree Absolute or a certified copy of The Final Judgment. The Decree Nisi is not accepted.

- If either party was married previously and widowed, an original or Certified copy of the Marriage Certificate and Death Certificate in respect of the deceased spouse.

- If either party has had a change of name, supporting documentation as applicable by Deed Pole or Adoption papers must be supplied.

- If the Bride and Groom have chosen to get married in a church, written confirmation from the Priest / Minister is required.

- Additional Court documentation is required for Civil Marriages.

- Persons under the age of 16 years cannot legally marry in Barbados.

- If the bride or groom is between the ages of 16 and 18 years, both parents must be present as they procure their legally required Marriage Licence, or evidence of parental consent is required in the form of an affidavit stamped by a notary public or a solicitor.

- Persons 18 years and older do not require parental consent.

- If there is any doubt as to either person's status in respect to the above, it may be necessary for an affidavit to be sworn in the presence of a local solicitor.

- Where necessary, all documents not in English must be accompanied by a certified translation.

- No Marriage Licence will be issued for a date beyond the expiry date of any visitor's stay in Barbados.

Couples will then be required to verbally verify that the information and documentation supplied is true and correct, and that each of them is legally free to marry the other.

Couples continue to choose Barbados for its romance, the hassle-free ease with which every aspect of their Destination Wedding can be arranged, whether chosen as a romantic get away for two – or the more traditional guest list of 100 or more, along with the lure of an exotic honeymoon. So if you have got the inclination, we have got the time. Time after time, after time. Imagine YOUR day... YOUR way... and start dreaming today... for you deserve your very own Wedding ... on the beautiful island paradise of Barbados!!

/ *Lisa Hutchinson*

above / a Barbadian 'Garden of Eden', Flower Forest, with 50 acres of dramatically landscaped tropical flora, sits on the western edge of the rugged Scotland District. The tranquillity of this garden, its breathtaking vistas of the east coast, majestic palm groves, spectacular heliconia and inquisitive monkeys will delight visitors

top / located on the south coast of Barbados, Graeme Hall Nature Sanctuary is home to the most diverse biodiversity and last significant mangrove wetland on the island. It features nature trails, large aviaries and educational facilities

left / all visitors are welcome to attend the Annual Flower and Garden Show, held in the early part of the year at their headquarters, Balls, Christ Church. The show provides an opportunity to see flowers and foliage at their best, particularly the recreation of their Chelsea exhibit. It is noteworthy that the Society has won 13 gold and six silver gilt medals since 1988 in this most prestigious show

The Natural World

above / the humble grapefruit – a little-known invention from Barbados

top / within 40 years of European settlement most of Barbados was transformed into sea of sugar cane

LIKE other islands of the West Indies, Barbados was once **densely forested** but within 40 years of European settlement most trees had been felled and the country transformed into a giant sea of **sugar cane**. Botanically, Barbados is part of the Lesser Antilles, an archipelago of small islands flanked by Puerto Rico in the north and Trinidad in the south. Some 2,100 species of flowering plants are native to the Lesser Antilles with 13 per cent unique or endemic to these islands. By comparison, Barbados is home to about 650 species of native and naturalized flowering plants, two of which are unique to Barbados. This relatively impoverished flora can be explained by the early land clearance for agriculture, the low-lying, coralline nature of the island with its limited ecological diversity and the fact that Barbados is much younger geologically than its volcanic neighbours.

For such a small spot on the earth, Barbados' flora is remarkably well documented, starting with Richard Ligon's *True and Exact History of the Island of Barbados* (1657). That island was very different to the one we know today, being described as "so grown with wood as there are no champions or savannas for men to dwell in". Many local plants are part of everyday Bajan life. The **maypole** *(Agave karatto)*, unique to Barbados and the Eastern Caribbean is one such, found in dry coastal areas. Fisherfolk use its flowering 'pole' as a float while diving for sea eggs (urchins), while youngsters scratch the names of their sweet hearts on the stiff, fleshy leaves. From a horticultural standpoint Barbados has given the world one of its most popular fruits. The **grapefruit**, originally called the rather ominous 'forbidden fruit', arose in Barbados as a hybrid of two Asian introductions, the sour orange and the

Bruce Hemming

above / some of Barbados' original forest still remains despite centuries of massive deforestation

top / Graeme Hall Nature Reserve

shaddock. No less a visitor than George Washington described eating this now widespread fruit, while visiting Barbados in 1751.

Like elsewhere in the world, a strong tradition of herbal medicine developed in Barbados. Barbadian **'bush teas'** combine the knowledge brought by slaves from Africa with elements of the European and Amerindian pharmacopoeia, as well as further expertise developed in the Caribbean. **Bitter melon cerasee** *(Momordica charantia)*, a kind of wild cucumber, is perhaps our best-known medicinal plant, widely respected as flu remedy.

Despite extensive development and intensive agriculture, a range of natural plant communities survives. These range from beach and dune vegetation to mangrove communities such as that of the **Graeme Hall Nature Reserve** on the south coast. Back from the beach, most of the littoral forest and dry woodland have long disappeared but, tucked away on a hillside in the northeast of the island, a 30-hectare tract of original forest, **Turner's Hall Wood**, has miraculously survived. Botanically, this is the most species-rich site on the island, with several plants that are found nowhere else in Barbados. This type of forest, comprising evergreen and deciduous trees and with few epiphytes, is too dry to be considered rainforest but it gives some idea of the tropical moist forest that in pre-Colombian times covered most of the country.

In fact, one positive aspect of the decline of 'King Sugar' is that areas that have fallen out of cultivation are gradually returning to forest. Of prime mention in this regard is the island's **gully network**, comprising chasms in the coral cap, up to 50 metres deep, and totalling some 450 km in length, with half of these forested. These also serve as watercourses from the high rainfall areas to the coast. In this sheltered environment, a unique forest community has developed comprising mainly native trees and shrubs. Woody vines bob and weave through the gully canopy, while the high humidity supports delicate sprays of ferns and mosses. One of the easiest ways to explore a Barbadian gully is to join the Sunday Walks, organized by the Barbados National Trust, an association committed to the preservation of the island's natural and man-made heritage.

Barbadians are, of course, great gardeners and a vast number of plants have been introduced to the island for their beauty. **Andromeda Botanic Gardens, Flower Forest** and **Orchid World** are public gardens with fine collections of exotic ornamentals.

Barbadian Fauna

With no dangerous snakes or other beasts to lose sleep over, unless you count the occasional centipede, you may well be lulled into thinking that there is no noteworthy animal life in Barbados. The only wild animals of any size in Barbados are both exotics, namely the green monkey and the mongoose. The **green monkey** *(Cercopithecus aethiops sabaeus)* was brought from West Africa some 350 years ago. Despite a bounty on its tail for all the crop damage it can cause, today an estimated 14,000 monkeys roam the island in small troops. A visit to the **Barbados**

above / black belly sheep

top / a green monkey at the Barbados Wildlife Reserve

Wildlife Reserve will guarantee you a close-up view of green monkeys.

We know a little more about the importation by the **mongoose** *(Herpestes javanicus)*. These were brought from India in the 1870s to control rats in the cane fields. Unfortunately, they soon turned their attention to other animals and are especially partial to fowls and their eggs, as many farmers know.

The other mammal to mention is the **North American raccoon** *(Procyon lotor)* that was once found in Barbados, living in caves, but now have disappeared.

While not an exciting wild beast, there is one large animal of the farm variety, which is uniquely Barbadian; the **black belly sheep**, which many northern visitors mistake for a goat, is a hybrid derived from an African hair sheep and the European wool sheep. It is a breed that developed on the island hundreds of years ago and provides the most tender, tasty lamb, more than can satisfy local demand.

A lack of adequate forest cover goes a long way in explaining the rather unimpressive bird fauna. There are probably 25 resident bird species, the best known being the **wood dove**, **blackbird** (grackle), **sparrow** and **yellow-breast**. However, besides these residents, over 150 species of migratory birds have been recorded using Barbados as a watering hole on their annual migration.

There may be no songbirds in Barbados but the pleasant 'ko-ki' sound, characteristic of nightfall in Barbados is thanks to the **whistling frog** *(Eleutherodactylus johnstonei)*. This indigenous species, no bigger than a fingernail and living in damp shady places, is also found in four other islands of the Eastern Caribbean. This is not to be confused with the **large toad** *(Bufo marinus)* called a frog or crapaud by most Bajans. This was introduced to the island in 1835 to control insect pests of sugar cane.

Of all animals, however, it is the reptiles that put Barbados on the map and qualify the Caribbean as a biodiversity hotspot. The tiny **blind snake** *(Leptotyphlops bilineata)* is the smallest snake in the world and is found only in St Lucia, Martinique and Barbados. It lives in leaf mould and might well be mistaken for a worm. The **racer snake** *(Liophis perfuscus)* is unique to Barbados, but was last seen in 1963 and, like the endemic Liophis species of both Grenada and Martinique, may also be extinct. The snake seen from time to time in the wetter parishes of Barbados and assumed until recently to be Liophis is, in fact, *Mastigodryas bruesi*, a snake also found in St Vincent, the Grenadines and Grenada. Barbadian lizards are also of note, with two of the six reported species unique to the island. One of the endemics is a gecko-like **lizard** *(Phyllodactylus pulcher)*, often found indoors. For two lizard species, *Kentropyx borckiana* and *Gymnophthalmus underwoodii*, males have never been seen and offspring are produced asexually by parthenogenesis or virgin birth! This surviving herpetofauna, with its relatively high endemism, is all the more remarkable for a geologically young island, and one that was virtually denuded of forest within a generation of settlement.

/ Sean Carrington

The Learning Curve – Education in Barbados

FOR Barbadians, education is considered to be of the utmost importance and has been accorded the highest priority by successive governments. In the 2004-2005 financial year almost 20 per cent of the national budget was spent on education.

In 1835 the British government started making an annual grant to Barbados and other Caribbean colonies for the education of the former enslaved blacks. The church, particularly the Anglican, became involved in providing elementary education.

Elementary education expanded during the century with an increasing number of schools being built in the various parishes. By the end of the 19th century the education system in Barbados was ahead of those in most of the other West Indian colonies.

A limited effort was also being made to provide some form of secondary education. In 1876 the three Central, three Higher and four Middle schools were accommodating about 200 pupils.

Today the Barbados system features three kinds of primary and secondary schools, the majority being government owned and maintained, whilst there are some private secondary schools which are government assisted, and some non-assisted or independent schools. The schools that are assisted by government receive grants and subventions that are generally used to pay the salaries of the teaching staff. The independent schools are primary schools, which charge fees to finance their operations.

> "By the end of the 19th century the education system in Barbados was ahead of those in most of the other West Indian colonies."

Primary Schools

Primary Schools cater for children in the 3-11 age group. There are 80 public primary schools located throughout the island with an enrolment of over 20,000 pupils. There are another dozen primary schools, which are run by private individuals. Well-trained and qualified teachers staff the primary schools, both public and private. Primary Schools are divided into infants' and junior departments. There is now an increasing emphasis on **Early Childhood Education** programmes and schools are equipping themselves to provide these.

The Primary School curriculum allows for the teaching of Language Arts, Mathematics, Science, Social Studies, Health and Family Life Education, Dance, Drama and Physical Education.

Pupils are prepared to write the **Barbados Secondary Schools Entrance Examination** (BSSEE), also known as the Common Entrance. It is taken by pupils who are 11 years of age and in their final year at Primary School. A few nine- and 10-year-old pupils also take this examination.

It is generally said that the system of primary education in Barbados has contributed to the extremely high literacy rate (98 per cent) recorded for the island.

There are some **special schools**, which are designed to cater to the needs of the hearing and visually impaired, and the mentally and physically challenged. The Irving Wilson and the Challenor School are two such institutions. Some primary schools, too, have programmes for special needs students.

Secondary Schools & Sixth-Form Schools

There are 23 public secondary schools of which 21 are co-educational. There is one single sex school for males and one for females. In addition there are seven private secondary schools equipped with the requisite facilities and a full complement of teachers.

There are over 22,000 students enrolled in the secondary schools of Barbados. Free education is available to those who attend government secondary schools. Students also obtain the requisite textbooks through a national Textbooks Loan Scheme. This scheme enables students to rent textbooks for an annual fee of Bds $75.

The Curriculum allows students to pursue studies in a number of areas: Humanities, Business Studies, Industrial Arts, Home Economics, Languages, Science and Fine Arts.

At Form Five most students write the **Caribbean Secondary Education Certificate Examination** (CSEC). Those who obtain passes in five or more subjects at the General Proficiency Level will be eligible to embark on studies at sixth-form schools or the Barbados Community College.

Four of the public Secondary Schools – Harrison College, Queen's College, Lodge and Combermere – offer sixth-form programmes. Students write the

Caribbean Advanced Proficiency Examinations (CAPE) in a number of subject areas. Students who achieve the highest grades in these examinations are awarded Barbados Scholarships and Exhibitions.

Higher Education

Since its establishment in 1968 the **Barbados Community College** has played a major role in the delivery of tertiary education on the island. The college attracts most of the graduates from fifth-form schools seeking post-secondary education. The BCC offers the Associate and Bachelor degree programme. At the College there are divisions of Health Sciences, Fine Arts, Hospitality studies, Science and Technology, Computer Studies Commerce, and Liberal Arts. The BCC programmes are diverse and provide students with the opportunity to study subjects other than the traditional ones. A grade-point average of 3.8 to 4.0 in the Associate Degree programme will earn a student a Barbados Scholarship or Exhibition.

The **Samuel Jackman Prescod Polytechnic** (opened in 1970) provides technical and vocational education. Courses are offered in over 25 disciplines ranging from Engineering to Cosmetology. Polytechnic graduates are prepared for employment in the agricultural, manufacturing and industrial sectors.

The future education of the island's children is assured by the **Erdiston Teachers' Training College** (opened in 1948). In recent years it has been restructured to enhance the quality of education through the delivery of pre-service, in-service and continuing education programmes for teachers and other stakeholders. Graduate Teachers who enrol at the College for professional training are awarded the **Diploma of Education** on successful completion of the course. Principals and other school administrators attend the College to complete the requirements for the **Certificate of Educational Management and Administration**.

At the apex of the system is the Cave Hill Campus of the **University of the West Indies**, established in 1963. The campus allows Barbadians to pursue first degrees and higher in various disciplines.

In addition Barbadian students can study at the other campuses of the University located at Mona, Jamaica, St Augustine, Trinidad and The Bahamas. The full economic cost of study for Barbadian nationals at UWI is borne by Government. The cooperation and support given by these institutions is remarkably strong and Barbados is in the enviable position of being able to provide a world-class education for its young citizens in several areas.

The location of a university campus in Barbados has been extremely significant, allowing Barbadian students the privilege of obtaining their degrees in their own country. These qualified Barbadians are able to contribute to their country's national development.

"The location of a university campus in Barbados has been extremely significant, allowing Barbadian students the privilege of obtaining their degrees in their own country. These qualified Barbadians are able to contribute to their country's national development."

Codrington School – enjoying a new lease of life

SET ON A HILL overlooking Consett Bay in the eastern, rural parish of St John, with a splendid vista of the Atlantic coast, is a small cluster of buildings in the shadow of the Anglican Church of the Holy Cross. These buildings seem to be the product of a bygone age – timeless and elegant in their restored form.

And indeed, they are, for these lovely buildings house a unique and treasured school in Barbados – Codrington. With its global perspective and international dimension, the school offers a very special education, not only to Barbadians but also to internationally mobile expatriate children who, for a few brief years, make Barbados their home.

Codrington began as a boarding school for girls in 1917 and there are still many 'old girls' from Barbados and all over the world, who have treasured memories of 'days of yore'. Indeed, adult 'Codrington girls' often dissolve into fits of laughter as they remember the pomp and the pranks of the boarding school of yesteryear.

Sadly, in the eighties, the 'old' Codrington closed its doors. It seemed that never again would the sound of ringing laughter from children at play be heard within those ancient walls. But, fortunately, there were people around who shared the 'Codrington Vision' and who were determined to see the school revived. In 2002, after two swift metamorphoses, the 'new' Codrington opened its doors, this time to boys as well as girls, offering a curriculum based on the highest standards of Barbadian and international education.

The pioneers of 2002 were led by the vision and determination of one woman, Sylvia Johnson, who is recognised as the founder of the new Codrington. Having been a teacher there in the 1970s, she shares a love for the place that seems to touch all who have been privileged to see the school in its pomp. Her efforts, and those of a group of like-minded people who shared a nostalgic belief that the school would rise again, saw that the doors opened again in September, 2002, to a small group of nine children.

Staffed by educators with internationally recognised qualifications, today Codrington offers children of primary and secondary school age an excellent educational programme.

With the introduction to the school of the methodology and philosophy of teaching and learning developed by the

International Baccalaureate Organisation (IBO), delivered by caring and dedicated teachers in small classes of approximately 12 students, Codrington students are exposed to national and international curricula, whilst receiving a high level of personal attention.

Set in three acres of wooded grounds, which include gardens and shady mahogany trees over a century old, Codrington is a registered charitable trust with three trustees and a seven-member board of governors. The headmaster, Dennison MacKinnon, a career teacher and administrator for more than 30 years, is also an acknowledged authority on the IB programme.

Codrington's custodians are justifiably proud of the school and are always happy to welcome visitors.

Further Educational opportunities

The **Barbados Institute of Management and Productivity** (BIMAP), which was established in 1971, offers services in the area of management training, consulting, research and small-business development to its members and clients. BIMAP specialises in management training. In recent years persons who graduate from the BIMAP programmes go on to study for higher degrees in Business, Marketing and Finance. The **University of Surrey** offers these degree programmes.

A **Skills Training** programme was started in 1979 and is designed for those who desire to enter the workforce as artisans, agriculturalists and apprentices. Meanwhile, the **Education Sector Enhancement Programme** also known as EDUTECH is an initiative by government to enhance the delivery of education in the island. The aims of the initiative are: the upgrading of schools through a civil-works programme; instituting curriculum reform; the training of teachers to be able to make use of new learning technologies; the provision of technological infrastructure that will prepare students to be proficient in the information age.

When the programme is fully implemented all schools on the island will be equipped with the necessary computer software and hardware to prepare students to function adequately and participate productively in the skill and information job market.

The Barbados government, the Inter-American Development Bank and the Caribbean Development Bank, finances this initiative, which is budgeted at US $213 million.

In Barbados every opportunity is given to students to help them succeed. Education is provided free of cost at the Primary, Secondary and Tertiary level. Bus fares are subsidised for primary and secondary school students. Those in attendance at secondary schools obtain their textbooks on loan. Daily lunches are provided for primary school pupils for which they pay a nominal fee.

Education in Barbados is always in a state of reform. A **University of Barbados** is to be established. This will be an amalgamation of the Barbados Community College, the Samuel Jackman Prescod Polytechnic and the Erdiston Teachers' Training College. The University of the West Indies and the Barbados government are working towards having a graduate in every household by 2015. Finally the Common Entrance Examination is to give way to a system of Continuous Assessment.

/ Martin Ramsay

"Every opportunity is given to students to help them succeed. Education is provided free of cost at the Primary, Secondary and Tertiary level."

Health Benefits
– A Model for
Others to Follow

IN THE mid-1980s, Barbadian health indicators showed that the overall health status of the country had improved substantially. In addition, by 1984 the government had taken major steps toward instituting a comprehensive healthcare service.

Barbados achieved considerable success in reducing its crude birth rate in the 1980s. **Mortality rates**, which had been steadily improving since 1974, deteriorated slightly in 1983. The death rate for the population rose in 1983 to 7.9 deaths per 1,000 inhabitants; much of the increase was attributed to a higher infant mortality rate, which rose 15 per cent to 24.5 deaths per 1,000 live births. This increase was caused largely by problems arising shortly after birth, particularly pneumonia and respiratory ailments. **Life expectancy** at birth in Barbados in 1983 was 70 years. Morbidity indicators in the 1980s approximated those found elsewhere in the Caribbean. Only 2.3 per cent of all deaths in 1982 were attributed to infectious and parasitic diseases. Statistics from that year indicated that two-thirds of all children aged one year and younger were inoculated against diphtheria, pertussis and tetanus and 53 per cent against measles.

In 1999, the mid-year **population** estimate was 267,400 persons, males (48 per cent) and females (52 per cent). The population under 15-years old was 22 per cent, while those over 65 years made up 12 per cent. The birth rate was 14.5 per thousand. Life expectancy at birth was 74.1 years for men and 79.1 years for women. The total **labour force** was approximately 135,500. At the end of 1999, the unemployment rate stood at 10.4 per cent. The average household size was 3.5 persons. Information also showed that 94 per cent had potable water supplied inside their houses, while the remaining 6 per cent had easy access to

Complementary Therapies in Barbados

CONSIDERING its small size, Barbados is remarkably well favoured in the diversity and wealth of its complementary practitioners. There are various therapies being practiced on the island, many with their own associations (some of which are listed below) ensuring that international standards are observed.

There is a definite trend worldwide towards combining strategies for optimum health. The complementary approach recognises the importance of 'prevention is better than cure' by encouraging a healthy lifestyle – that is, taking care of diet, exercise, mental and emotional well being – and establishing a harmonious environment, to the extent possible. Biofeedback has proven that relaxation is key to good health and many complementary approaches, such as meditation, massage, reflexology and reiki, aim to bring the client into a peaceful state of mind.

However, when good health breaks down, the complementary approach allows maximum benefit to the individual as both conventional and other therapies can be used.

These are some, but not all of the modalities available to

visitors and residents alike: acupressure, acupuncture, aromatherapy, chiropractic, clinical kinesiology, clinical nutritional microscopy, colonics, craniosacral, herbalism, homeopathy, iridology, osteopathy, sports massage, reflexology, reiki, shiatsu, tai chi / qigong, therapeutic massage and yoga.

Barbados is blessed with a wonderful environment for creating a magical holiday. Its pristine beaches – ideal for relaxing and meditating – clean seas for swimming and snorkelling, hiking trails in unspoiled nature areas and energy vortex, induce calm and contentment. With the added plus of being able to access specialty therapies and dedicated therapists, this little parcel of land at the edge of the Atlantic, satisfies the conventional as well as the eclectic traveller – a bit like complementary therapy itself!

/ Verity Dawson

potable water supplies. In addition, more than 75 per cent of households had a telephone service and over 90 per cent had electricity installed. Improved water and sewage disposal was credited with the decline of morbidity rates from 1974 to 1985. The completion in 1982 of the sewage system in the capital city of Bridgetown dramatically improved the urban sanitation situation. A similar system was completed in 2002 for the south coast (one of the two main tourist belts) and plans are under way to have a west coast sewage system completed by 2010. The rest of the island depends on septic tanks for waste disposal.

The consistently improving health conditions in Barbados were the direct result of government efforts to enact a healthcare programme. Between 1978 and 1983, Ministry of Health expenditure, including social security, represented an average of 14.5 per cent of total government outlay. The government planned delivery of free healthcare to all Barbadians through two basic programmes, the **General Practitioner Service** and the **Barbados Drug Service**. The former was designed to bring medical services to virtually all areas of the island, but it had not been fully implemented. The Barbados Drug Service began operations in 1980 and improved the delivery of prescription and over-the-counter drugs, providing increased efficiency and reduced costs.

The mission statement of the Barbados Drug Service is 'To provide quality pharmaceuticals to all residents of Barbados at an affordable price and to serve the beneficiaries in a courteous and efficient manner'. Quite a mouthful! However, they have been able to achieve this for the past 26 years, despite several obstacles. Drugs listed in the Barbados Drug Formulary are provided free at private participating pharmacies to children under 16, persons with some chronic non-communicable disease and those 65 years and older. Antenatal care for pregnant mothers before the 12th week of gestation and health services for adolescents are provided at public polyclinics.

Barbados healthcare facilities include one general hospital, **Queen Elizabeth's Hospital**, one psychiatric facility, the **Psychiatric Hospital**, district hospitals, polyclinics and health centres. Queen Elizabeth's Hospital and the Psychiatric Hospital each contain approximately 630 beds. The School of Clinical Medicine and Research of the UWI is based at the QEH, which is used for teaching and research. Services at eight polyclinics are located strategically within easy access of the catchment areas they serve. Healthcare services at government facilities are free of cost. The private healthcare market, comprised of more than 100 general practitioners and a similar number of consultants, is growing. There are also private sector laboratories, radiological and diagnostic services available. The private **Bayview Hospital** provides 30 acute-care beds while 37 private nursing and senior citizens' homes provide long-term care for the elderly. The polyclinics are supplied with the necessary equipment for the delivery of quality healthcare. There is a referral system between clinics, hospitals, the private sector and other support services. Public health services include: family health, such as maternal and child health; adolescent health; community mental health; dental health; nutrition;

"Japan and Barbados are at the top of global rankings of nations with most centenarians per capita."

below / living tradition – the
marching band of the West India
Regiment wearing Zouave uniform

general practice clinics; environmental health services such as food hygiene, mosquito and rodent control.

During the period 1997-1999, the crude mortality rate declined from 9.3 to 8.3 per thousand. By 1999 diseases of pulmonary circulation and other forms of heart disease had moved into first position, replacing cerebrovascular disease as the leading cause of death. Diabetes and ischemic heart disease remained in third and fourth places.

The new millennium saw the privatization of the management of Queen Elizabeth Hospital in an effort to improve efficiency. It is still too early to tell the merits of such a decision.

Japan and Barbados are at the top of global rankings of nations with most centenarians per capita. One thing is clear; Barbados has established a framework for the delivery of healthcare that is designed to provide equity and quality.

/ Andrel Griffith

Law and Order

FOR MANY Caribbean people Barbados epitomizes Law and Order to the maximum. Other countries in the region can look on only in admiration of its law-abiding society, one in which political opponents are not threatened, its citizens do not carry illegal weapons on their person or scream obscenities at members of its police force. Here, the law brings with it order.

It is a Caribbean aphorism that 'in Barbados people are so law-abiding that they say to their enemies, "I leave you in the hands of the Lord", meaning 'I will not fight with you or harm you. Rather, I will wait for God to wreak vengeance on you'. However, although Barbadians are, by and large, a peaceful people, they are also extremely aware of their rights under the law and are just as likely as any other Caribbean people to hire a lawyer to sue you if, peradventure, you infringe their rights. There are more **lawyers** per capita in Barbados than in any other CARICOM territory (one to every 700 persons), there are also more lawyers resident here than in any other territory except Jamaica, Trinidad and Tobago and Guyana (some 400-odd lawyers are listed in the telephone directory). They all belong to the **Barbados Bar Association**, a vibrant body, led by Wilfred Abrahams, a young lawyer.

Furthermore, everywhere you go in Barbados you are never far from a lawyer's office. Once they all had their Chambers or offices in the city of Bridgetown, but now that that there is housing and industrial settlements even in the hinterland parishes of Saint Lucy, Saint Andrew, Saint Philip, Saint Joseph and Saint John, law offices are popping up all over the place.

Not only do you have lawyers' offices in each of the 11 parishes, but there are now **police stations** and sub-stations in every parish except Saint John (our

> *"Other countries in the region can look on only in admiration of its law-abiding society."*

Willie Alleyne

count reveals 14 such stations, including the Police Headquarters at the Central Police Station in the city of Bridgetown, one at Port St Charles, another at the Airport and one at the Bridgetown Harbour.

Then there are 14 **Magistrates Courts**, including a special one at Station Hill. These courts deal with criminal, civil, family and traffic cases as Courts of First Instance. Next there are the **High Courts**, then the **Courts of Appeal** and Finally the **Supreme Court** presided over by the Chief Justice, His Honour, Sir David Simmons, QC, Knight of St Andrew.

Sir David, a London-trained lawyer is a forward-looking Chief Justice, who has helped to pilot the new (2005) **Caribbean Court of Justice**. Himself a former Attorney-General of Barbados, he looks forward to the new Hall of Justice and modernisation of the Barbados Justice System.

However, if you believe, perhaps, that these represent the sum total of the island's processes and apparatus when it comes to law enforcement, you would not be correct. Barbados has Juvenile Courts for those persons less than 16 years of age; it has Juvenile Correction Facilities (commonly called **Dodds** and **Summervale**), which are Reform Schools for 'wayward' boys and girls respectively. It also has a Probation Office to deal with girls who wander and boys who stray from the straight and narrow.

There is a **Police Task Force** to deal with very serious crime or situations of national crisis, and a **Criminal Investigation Department**. There is a Neighbourhood Police programme, mounted police patrols, mobile patrols, Special Branch and foot patrols in every parish and there is now a protocol that permits the implementation of joint patrols, consisting of Special Branch police officers and select crack troops from the **Barbados Defence Force**. Speaking of the Defence Force, that agency is Barbados' first line of protection against smuggling on the sea, through its Coast Guard section and, of course, the BDF itself is a full-fledged army, having come into being in 1979 and having won its spurs in the October 1983 rescue mission in Grenada, alongside the forces of the USA and Britain.

Barbados has a large double-gender **penitentiary** at Harrison's Point, Saint Lucy, once the base for the US Navy, this complex now serves a different area of security (the old one at Glendairy, Station Hill, Saint Michael was burnt down in a rare prison riot in 2005). However, that is a temporary facility because a brand new state-of-the-art correctional facility is under construction at Summervale, St Philip, next to the current juvenile reform agencies.

Completing the picture, there are the **Customs and Immigration** Departments at our major ports of entry and Barbados is the Headquarters of the **Regional Security Service**, which combines and coordinates the security forces of the CSM countries.

Of course Barbados is NOT crime free (which country is?), but it is one of the safest countries in the hemisphere. Are you surprised?

/ *Trevor Marshall*

opposite top / mounted police parade in Heroes' Square, Bridgetown

opposite bottom / the Barbados Defence Force was established in 1979, and has provided invaluable support locally and regionally in areas of security assistance, maritime law enforcement, disaster relief and in ceremonial duties. The principle units of the BDF are the Barbados Regiment, the Barbados Coast Guard and the Barbados Cadet Corps

above / a selection of the newspapers and magazines currently published in Barbados

The Media

BARBADOS is well served for information, boasting two newspapers, two radio stations and several magazines. The first newspaper published in Barbados was the **Barbados Gazette**. Started by American David Harry, from Philadelphia, it first appeared on October 9, 1731, and continued until at least 1792.

Another newspaper, the **Barbados Mercury** was first published in 1762, and ran until after 1848. In the 19th century several newspapers flourished, chief of which was **The Liberal**, edited for some 25 years by **Samuel Jackman Prescod**, who became one of Barbados' national heroes. In the 1870s there were no fewer than five newspapers on the island as well as a number of other publications, which were stimulated by the **Confederation Crisis**.

By 1895 Barbados received its first major newspaper, the **Barbados Advocate** that is still published after 111 years in the form of a daily paper. Other newspapers have been **The Herald**, founded in 1919, **The Observer**, founded by Wynter Crawford in 1934 and the **Daily News**, established in 1961. By far the most popular newspaper of all time is **The Nation** that began as a weekly paper in 1973, but is now published as a national daily. Both the Barbados Advocate and The Nation newspapers provide daily coverage of local and international news.

There are about 10 **radio stations** operating in Barbados. The Government-owned **Caribbean Broadcasting Corporation** operates CBC radio 900, Q100.7 FM and Liberty 98.1 FM, while the **Starcom Network Corporation** is responsible for Voice of Barbados 92.9 FM, Hott 95.3 FM, Love104.1 FM and 790 AM. The Broadcasting Service, a private entity, operates two more stations, BBS FM 90.7 and Faith 102 FM. The mass communication students at the **Barbados Community College** also broadcast on an FM frequency.

above / the offices of the Caribbean Broadcasting Corporation in Barbados

The most popular mass communication medium on this island is the radio. Radio has influenced the habits of Barbadians and residents who have always organized their daily lives around the sounds coming either from their Rediffusion box (cable box, up to the 1970s) or the AM/FM radio networks (in more recent decades).

The youth of today all groove to the sounds played by local disc jockeys, as well as those coming from North America, Jamaica and Trinidad and Tobago. Modern artistes such as **Rihanna**, **Rupee**, **Edwin Yearwood**, and **Alison Hinds** as well as Jamaican Reggae artistes are very popular. However, the more mature citizens utilize radio for news, views and enlightenment. The **talk show** is by far the most popular type of programme and for Barbadians a most welcome conduit by which to express their views on every matter under the sun.

The Caribbean Broadcasting Corporation operates the lone television station on a 24-hour basis. This corporation also offers subscribers access to **Multi-Choice**, a cable television service featuring some 69 North American channels and networks, also on a 24-hour basis. **Starcom Network**, its main competitor, offers **Direct TV**, which also brings North American television fare to the Barbadian viewer. Together these two companies take viewers into the 21st-century world of instant news, views and entertainment. There are also regional media stations, such as **CMC** and the **CANA** news service.

At present media workers in Barbados are a relatively small coterie, who have skills in a number of communication arenas (radio, internet, print journalism and television). However, they are not united in one body as was the case in the mid-1990s when **CAMWORK** (Caribbean Media Workers) was flourishing as a union, with regional columnist Rickey Singh, an influential figure of international fame, leading the media workers on the island. However, the fame of some journalists, such as renowned cricket commentator and writer Tony Cozier, ensures respect.

Undoubtedly the media sectors in Barbados are undergoing a major transformation with emphasis on developing infrastructure and the skill level of the workforce. There is a heavy emphasis on training new recruits at the **Barbados Community College** and at **UWI**, Mona Jamaica. This is because the two major challenges facing the media are the cost of international communications, which are perceived as being too high, and an inadequate supply of appropriately-trained personnel. There is a general acceptance that reliable cost-competitive communications is a pre-requisite for future growth in the media sector.

As the Barbados media managers look to the future they can assure themselves that in terms of radio, television, newspaper and internet services, they provide a high quality service to the Barbadian consumer and that their offerings are penetrating the region. Ultimately the media in Barbados prides itself on being effective, efficient members of 'the Fourth Estate' and on maintaining Barbados' reputation for intellectually stimulating and tasteful coverage of all that is newsworthy, novel and progressive on this island.

/ Trevor Marshall

"Ultimately the media in Barbados prides itself on being effective, efficient members of 'the Fourth Estate' and on maintaining Barbados' reputation for intellectually stimulating and tasteful coverage of all that is newsworthy, novel and progressive on this island."

Apes Hill Club: on a par with the best

WHILE Barbados climbs the ladder to becoming one of the Caribbean's premier golf destinations, the Apes Hill Club has joined in on the venture with a project boasting a superb new facility that will appeal enormously to the golf and polo community.

Apes Hill Club is a partnership between Sir Charles Williams, the owner of the largest construction company in Barbados and the Landmark Land Company, one of the most prestigious community, golf and resort developers in the world.

Construction has already begun on the dramatic 470-acre site to coax a picturesque and challenging golf course from one of the most beautiful sugar estates in Barbados. When complete, Apes Hill Club will offer a diverse range of indoor and outdoor facilities designed to provide a quality, relaxed lifestyle for its residents.

The 18-hole golf course will be as fine as there is in the Caribbean. It has been designed skilfully to take full advantage of its beautiful environment, which boasts an expansive area of rolling hills, wooded gullies, rocky outcrops, old quarries and small lakes. The designers at Landmark Land have also taken full advantage of its elevated position, which offers magnificent panoramic views overlooking both the west and east coasts of Barbados.

The impressive Waterhall Polo Centre that is already in operation gives residents the opportunity to watch world-class international polo right on their doorstep. Residents can also benefit from expert coaching in this exciting sport or simply enjoy the excellent riding facilities.

There will be a hotel on site as well as a clubhouse that will have a restaurant and bar, modern fitness facilities and a swimming pool. Also included will be a tennis centre with all three playing surfaces (clay, grass and hard) and a lavish full-service spa, appealing to all the senses aimed at rejuvenating mind, body and spirit. Other activities will include croquet, lawn bowling and, of course, sun bathing.

People who enjoy natural beauty, golf, tennis, polo or just relaxing will love what Apes Hill Club has to offer. The elegant yet challenging golf course will attract golfers of all levels, while the other amenities can provide constant entertainment. To accommodate those not so fluent in all things Barbadian, the Apes Hill Club Concierge Service will help homeowners discover the island at their own pace, as well as ensuring that everything for themselves and their family is taken care of.

When complete, the Apes Hill Club Community will have 200 single-family homes and 200 villas ranging in size, from a third of an acre to 1.25 acres. Most of these lots are not only located on the golf course but also have breathtaking views of the coastlines.

The philosophy of Landmark Land over the last 35 years has been to find special properties with inherent beauty and natural characteristics and develop them in a way that retains these qualities and protects the natural environment, while creating a unique lifestyle for its residents.

Landmark is known for its world-class golf facilities, having built the 'best new course of the year' and the 'best new international course of the year' in the last five years. Five of their courses are listed amongst the top 100 courses in the world. The company has built many of America's finest, including the Ocean Course at Kiawah Island, Oak Tree Golf Club and multiple courses at PGA West. These golf clubs have hosted many highly significant international golf tournaments, including the Ryder Cup, the World Cup and The PGA Championship. Landmark rates Apes Hill as one of the very best natural environments that they have ever had the pleasure of working on.

National Progress and Development

THE NATIONAL progress and development of Barbados is founded in the traditions of a small-island people with a progressive worldview.

While still maintaining a warm and personal approach to business, Barbados embraces serious change in a new-world order, open to all comers. The presence of the nation at the world's negotiating tables demands that Barbados complies with accepted practices on free trade and movement of people and recognises that in order to survive, competitiveness and standards must be high. This approach has so far placed Barbados amongst the nations with the highest **Human Development Index** (HDI) as defined by the United Nations. An index of '30' places Barbados amongst the top 20 per cent of nations in terms of the well-being of its citizens – as manifested in high life expectancy, literacy, education, and healthy childbirth, and also in a high standard of supporting physical infrastructure.

The **communications infrastructure** in Barbados allows the sharing of knowledge and experience with others at a level that equals or surpasses levels in countries such as France and Canada. More than half the population of Barbados uses telephone landlines and the internet while about three quarters of the population subscribes to cell phones. High-speed wireless services complete the suite of services increasingly used by individuals and establishments, thereby encouraging a diverse array of communications ranging from down-to-earth conversations between Bajans trading recipes for salt fish and coucou, to complex international business transactions.

Transactions in **the offshore sector** have boosted development in Barbados since the late 1990s when this economic activity supplemented the export of sugar as

> *"The Human Development Index, as defined by the United Nations, places Barbados amongst the top 20 per cent of nations in terms of the well-being of its citizens."*

Willie Alleyne

above / Caribbean Lifestyles Ltd is a well-established property development company with a proven track record of connecting people worldwide with the ultimate tropical places to live and play. At Caribbean Lifestyles, they live by the ethos of 'Fine Homes for Modern Living'

top / the redevelopment of the Kensington Oval to host the 2007 Cricket World Cup Final

left / from its inception, Realtors Ltd has determined to give that extra special personalised service to all of their clients. It is the reason they remain at the top of the real estate game in Barbados. They represent 122 villas and offers short and long-term rentals, sales, property management, valuations and insurance

a major earner of foreign exchange. Well-established and well-regulated offshore sectors offer international business company registration, banking, management of trusts and mutual funds, insurance products, and registration of US foreign sales corporations.

Sugar-based products and services remain the primary agricultural industry. The industry is now being re-structured to include a diversity of uses for the cane as well as the sugar itself. Under the restructuring plan, the island's sugar production will be carried out at one new factory instead of the three factories currently in operation. The new factory will begin producing by-products of ethanol and bagasse (cane trash) for generating electricity by January 2008, as well as branded sugar for the local market and speciality sugar for export. One of the existing factories at Buckley, St George, will be converted into a living museum focussing on the nation's 300-year-old sugar industry,

Another museum-in-the making is the **Barbados Cricket Museum** that has been described by Dr Trevor Carmichael, President of the Barbados Museum and Historical Society, as a way of recognising cricket as, "An important institution in its galvanising of inner social cohesion and its external popularisation of the Island". The 2007 presence in Barbados of the **Cricket World Cup** (CWC) provides an opportunity for the genesis of such a museum to complement the refurbished **Kensington Oval**, which has already received a face-lift worth Bds $30 million so that the ground will be fit to host the final. At this time of writing, over two billion fans overseas are expected to join, via satellite, the 27,000 who will be packed into Kensington. The CWC is third in popularity as a world-class sporting event, after the Summer Olympics and FIFA Football World Cup. Action will be broadcast and reported on by 400 journalists from a new media centre at the southern end of the ground.

The **Golf World Cup** at one of Barbados' premier golf destinations, the Sandy Lane Golf Resort, precedes the Cricket World Cup, in 2006. Noted golfing architect Tom Fazio has recently undertaken renovations to the golf courses that now offer a choice between a 9-hole and two 18-hole championship courses. Champion golfer, Tiger Woods brought international attention to this superb location when he married his sweetheart, Elin Nordegren, at the Sandy Lane Clubhouse in 2004. The couple spent the time before and after their wedding much like other visitors, sightseeing, swimming, snorkelling and sailing around the island.

Celebrity visits like these, highlight the regard with which all visitors hold the island in terms of the natural resources and hospitality, and the infrastructure that allows them to enjoy a home away from home. Caribbean breezes, sparkling seas, and other natural treasures, are shared with Barbadians who love to make visitors feel welcome. Cultural activities such as the Crop Over Festival and the Oistins Fish Fry, exciting nightlife, sun-drenched days, and natural heritage sites such as Harrisons Cave, Folkestone Marine Reserve, and Carlisle Bay near the capital city of Bridgetown, all attract more than one million visitors to Barbados each year.

"Over two billion fans overseas are expected to join, via satellite, the 27,000 who will be packed into Kensington Oval."

Co-operators General Insurance Company Ltd was established in 1993. It is owned by the Credit Union movement in Barbados. The company writes predominantly motor, residential and commercial property business. Its Board of Directors, management and staff are committed to providing trusted financial protection to the credit union movement and the wider Barbadian public. Their mission is to be the leader in providing high quality customer service with innovative insurance products at competitive prices and to achieve consistent and satisfactory returns to its shareholders

above / Armstrong Agencies Ltd offer a full import, wholesale, distribution and marketing service in Barbados. They also offer transshipment to other Caribbean islands. Their well-trained staff bring decades of experience, expertise and dedication to the company

top / Tropical Shipping is one of the leading containerised cargo carriers in the Caribbean region. From its headquarters at the Port of Palm Beach, Tropical, which is owned by Nicor Inc (NYSE:GAS), currently serves 33 ports throughout the Bahamas, Caribbean and South America

left / Laparkan (Barbados) Limited, a subsidiary of Laparkan Trading, specialises in sea and airfreight. They are capable of responding to their clients' needs for frequent, versatile and cost effective import and export of general cargo and removal services. Dedicated to providing a quality service, with their knowledge of Barbados and of international customs requirements they can help their customers through the process of relocating. Their operations include import customs clearance, delivery to any residence or business islandwide and the provision of labour to facilitate the move

above / Automotive Art was started in 1990. Beginning with a staff of just six, co-founders Dereck Foster and Hugh Blades have successfully grown the company in just 16 years to a staff of 140 at its HQ in Barbados, where it operates three stores. The business has expanded beyond the shores of Barbados, becoming the region's largest auto-care retailer, operating in over 20 countries throughout the Caribbean, Central and South America. Automotive Art is a one-stop automotive superstore and service centre offering a wide choice of quality brands including accessories, batteries, car-care products, paint and ancillaries, tools, tyres, wheels, motorcycles, electronics and the services to install them

right / Moore Paragon (Caribbean) Limited is a regional, premier full-service provider of print and related services, including document-based business process outsourcing. For over 35 years they have been serving customers in retail, technology, financial services, manufacturing, healthcare and many other industries. Their products include solutions in commercial printing, direct mail, statement processing, labels, stock and custom rolls, warehousing and forms management

Willie Alleyne

above / for over 20 years Jennifer Alleyne Ltd has provided personalised service in villa sales, luxury villa rentals and property management. Their portfolio includes some of the finest properties on the island, so whether it is beachfront apartment or something on the golf course, they can help find a property to suit most needs

top / how would you like to live here, at the Lakes Development? You can! A wide variety of villas and apartments are available, suited to full-time residents with benefits tailored to the over 55s, the second home buyer – with a 'lock up and go' service or rental pool option – and the property investor. With prices starting at US$320,000, purchases come on freehold or lifetime leasehold with guaranteed cash back plan

left / Grantley Adams International Airport Terminal

Approximately half of these visitors arrive as passengers on cruise ships, while the other half arrive by air. The seaport and airport are both international hubs for travellers. The man-made **Deep Water Harbour** in Bridgetown has been designed to accommodate the largest cruise ships on the seas today, as well as ships carrying sugar and other cargo. A major program of expansion and reform costing Bds $100 million is ongoing to ensure the port's continuing status as 'best in class'. By far the biggest project in this program is a Bds $40 million joint venture to build a new cruise pier to increase the port's daily passenger handling capacity by about 8,000.

The **Grantley Adams International Airport Terminal** has also been the subject of a major program of expansion designed to enhance the traveller's experience. The new Arrivals Terminal adds more than 70,000 square feet of floor space to the airport, providing 50 per cent more space for immigration processing. The new baggage claim area is almost twice the size of the old facility, and the new departure lounge offers passengers greater comfort, with easy access to an expanded retail concourse. Perhaps the most striking design features of the airport expansion project are the peaked membrane tent roofs, which allow natural light to filter into the terminal by day, thus reducing energy costs.

The spiralling costs of energy are not only a concern at the airport but also a universal concern that Barbadians are addressing by way of a new **National Energy Policy**. This policy focuses on the oil and natural gas that are currently the main sources of energy used in Barbados and on the alternatives – particularly solar power and biofuels. Solar water heating has long been popular in Barbados and now there is a move towards solar-powered vehicles led by William Hinds in his **Solar Shuttles**. These shuttles are demonstration vehicles that conduct sightseeing tours around Bridgetown, simultaneously enthusing passengers with the potential for solar power. Handel Callender of Native Sun NRG, is like Hinds, a pioneer in **alternative fuels**. Currently he manufactures biodiesel on a small-scale at the Future Centre in St Thomas. The biodiesel is created from used vegetable oil collected mainly by students at the Lester Vaughan Secondary School, and also from interested businesses and agencies.

Plans for the expansion of both initiatives in alternative energy, and plans by the Government of Barbados to establish a **wind farm,** are ongoing and show considerable promise but, until the time arrives that they are well established, Barbados remains dependent on oil and gas. Barbados is one of the few islands in the Caribbean with oil and natural gas fields within its territory, and supplies are used locally to decrease the need to import some of the island's fuel. Natural gas consumption is in the order of 30 million cubic metres annually, so the proved national reserves of 141.6 million cubic metres, as of January 1, 2002 could be depleted very soon. Discussions between Barbados and petroleum-rich Trinidad and Tobago, regarding the potential of an undersea gas pipeline, are well advanced. Similarly, discussions between the Government of Barbados and several international oil exploration companies are underway. Oil production from Barbados' own fields is approximately 1,000 barrels per day, whereas

"Perhaps the most striking design features of the airport expansion project are the peaked membrane tent roofs, which allow natural light to filter into the terminal by day, thus reducing energy costs."

above / the Barbados International Business Promotion Corporation (BIBPC) is the principal business development agency in the government's efforts to position Barbados as a leading financial services centre and a first-rate domicile for local and international investment. As a prime international business centre, Barbados has many attractive features that combine to make it a unique and viable location for business. Companies setting up in Barbados are able to achieve their international business objectives by operating in a compelling mix of a strong economy, a low tax environment, skilled and enthusiastic human resources and an enabling world-class professional environment, inclusive of legal, banking and accounting services. BIBPC promotes and facilitates foreign direct investment in Barbados and is responsible for the creation of new products and the identification of appropriate opportunities within key global jurisdictions

left / Founded in 1971, Brooks LaTouche Photography is one of Barbados' leading photo studios. Fully digitalised; it boasts an extensive cricket library and a full range of photo services catering to its clients in Barbados and the wider Caribbean. This spacious air-conditioned studio is fully equipped for portrait and commercial work, with changing room facilities and ample client parking

above / Eric Hassell & Son Ltd is a family-owned shipping agency, stevedore contractor and international freight forwarder, handling over 400 vessels per annum. With a guiding philosophy to provide the most honest, efficient and hassle-free service available, the company currently represent various bulk carriers, container lines and worldwide NVOCC operators

right / Stansfeld Scott is a professional marketing and distribution company with a premium portfolio of leading fine wines, spirits, beverages and consumer products. Their success has come through long-term commitment and persistence, as well as a proactive approach to product development and customer service. It has earned the company wide support in the trade and a high level of consumer confidence

above / Innotech Services Ltd is a family-owned group of companies operating in Barbados and the Caribbean region since 1992. As a reputable and dynamic contracting organisation, Innotech undertakes construction projects in all sectors of the industry, including residential, industrial, commercial, civil and tourist

top / operating through its local office based at White Park, St Michael, ILLUMINAT provides local and regional solutions in Information, Communication and Technology (ICT) to Governments, businesses and institutions. The company has strong partnerships with leading international names, including Microsoft, Hewlett Packard, Avaya and Oracle, which allow it to offer the latest solutions to its valued customers

left / IBM Barbados is a significant part of the IBM Caribbean organisation that extends from Guyana in the south to Bermuda in the north, and encompassing all the English and Dutch speaking Caribbean Islands. As a branch office of IBM, the organisation in Barbados has fast and ready access to industry specialists, experts and consultants within IBM Canada and worldwide, all with the same IBM values of dedication to their clients' success and innovation

consumption is about 10 times as much. Barbados currently imports oil from Venezuela and Trinidad and Tobago, and is looking to discover more reserves offshore.

Just as petroleum reserves are important, so too are reserves of fresh water. This reality is especially significant during the dry season between December and May when reserves become low. Special joint programs involving Government and the private sector are ongoing in the implementation of **water conservation**. The Barbados Water Authority, Environmental Protection Department and Ministry of Tourism are collaborating to implement a Water Conservation and Management Project in the Tourism and Hotel Sector. Two sewerage projects are in progress, one to serve the south coast and the other the west coast. The treatment plant for the south coast has been completed and work is ongoing for house connections. Work on the West Coast Sewerage Project commenced in 2002. Also of significance is the 30,000 metres cubed per day Reverse Osmosis Desalination Plant, constructed in 2000 to desalinate brackish water to augment the potable water supplies.

The same intensity of focus and expertise that is being devoted to the management of energy sources and fresh water is also being devoted to the management of solid waste in Barbados. This issue poses a serious challenge in a small island with a resident population of about 270,000 and an annual influx of over one million visitors. The first line of approach is through the implementation of a waste minimisation programme supported by a strong education programme. Focus on waste is supplemented by research into such aspects as linking waste management to energy creation. Subjects of research are the collection of landfill gases in order to create energy, as well as large-scale composting to reduce waste and harmful greenhouse gases. Such activities are part of the infrastructural Integrated Solid Waste Management Programme, which is absolutely critical to the social and economic development of Barbados.

Also critical to the development of Barbados – and to the basic sanity of road users – is yet another infrastructural project dubbed '**Operation Freeflow**'! This whimsically-named, yet seriously intentioned, three-year project includes the widening of the key ABC highway at certain points, construction of underpasses in critical areas, erection of six flyovers, synchronisation of traffic lights and the building of a park-and-ride system. Launched in July 2006, Operation Freeflow is not intended to create an expressway, such as those in the more speedy parts of North America or Europe. For after all is said and done, the internationalism that is embraced so enthusiastically by Barbadians is still tempered by an easy-going speed and neighbourly greeting as each driver shares the road with another.

/ *Susan Mahon*

above / Barbados Packaging Industries Ltd is the distribution office of Caribbean Packaging Industries, manufacturers of corrugated cartons and packaging materials. As the smallest member of the multinational packaging group, Canadian Overseas Packaging Industries, BPI plays a key role in 'packaging the business of Barbados', providing packaging for all sectors of the economy

"After all is said and done, the internationalism that is embraced by Barbadians is still tempered by an easy-going speed and neighbourly greeting as each driver shares the road with another."

The Political History of Barbados

FEW PEOPLE that come to Barbados on holiday stop to consider the politics of the island with all its complexity and intrigue. For most tourists Barbados is a cluster of beaches, accommodation and entertainment facilities, but all this needs to be managed and as a result there is also a **rich political history** that should be considered. Interestingly, the politics of Barbados is not dissimilar to the politics of most other developed countries and as such our political history has witnessed similar developments over the years.

The last century will no doubt be recorded as one that toggled between two sides of the political and **ideological continuum** globally. There was the political empire, typical at the commencement of the 20th century and associated with a narrowly-defined democracy and a tradition of conquest, as was the case in the United Kingdom and Russia under the Tsar. By the middle of the century, however, democracies had been established throughout the world and several of these empires had given way to **decentralisation** and ultimately independence. Ironically, as the century drew to a close, the phenomenon known as **globalisation** threatened to re-establish undemocratic global empires and return the world to a political state reminiscent of the beginning of the 1900s.

This global synopsis is useful as a backdrop against which a brief historical sketch of Barbadian politics could take place since, here too, we have seen a continuum. In 1900, Barbados was part of an empire with very little say in the running of its own affairs. Ironically, a combination of globalisation and the impact of international financial institutions has ensured that at the end of the century, we have once more relinquished all but de jure control of our affairs.

In the meantime, however, there have been interesting developments on our

The Magnificent Seven: The Premiers and Prime Ministers of Barbados, 1946-2006

BARBADOS has been well served over the past 60 years by a succession of men of renown as Premiers and then Prime Ministers. Following the civil disturbances of July 1937, there was a new "wind of change" blowing through the society and by the next year, 1938, the oldest political party in the British Caribbean, the Barbados Labour Party was founded and by the end of that year Grantley Adams had become its leader and President. This was the beginning of mass democracy in this island and over the next 68 years, Barbados was served by Adams himself and Dr Hugh G Cummins as Premiers. Then came Errol Barrow and his revolutionary concept of Independence which was achieved in 1966. He was followed in succession by J M G M "Tom" Adams, son of Sir Grantley, then Harold B St John and Barrow himself for a second term.

Barrow's death, 21 years after Independence, catapulted Erskine Sandiford into the highest elected office and he has been succeeded by Owen Arthur, who has been at the helm of Barbados' political ship over the past 12 years.

Here are Barbados' Magnificent Seven! 1946 - 2006

Premiers

The Right Excellent Sir Grantley Herbert Adams, Kt. (1957), C.M.G. (1953), C.B.E (1951). Q.C (1953), M.P.; legislator, barrister-at-law; Chairman Barbados Labour Party. Born at "Colliston," Government Hill 28th April, 1898, Son of Fitzherbert Adams and his wife Rose, nee Turney. Educated at St. Giles (Primary), Harrison College (Secondary), Oxford University (Island Scholar). Married Grace nee Thorne: 1 son. Career: Editor "Agricultural Reporter", 1927-30; formerly,

Pres. Barbados Progressive League, President Workers Union, President Labour Party, Caribbean Labour Congress; mem. U.K. Delegation to U.N; Paris 1948; member. Exec. C'ttee, 1946 - 54; Premier of B'dos, 1954 - 58; "Father of Political Democracy" and "Father of Franchise Reform".

Prime Minister of the West Indies Federation, 1958-62; rep. B'dos at several conferences in the West Indies, England, Europe; formerly Editor of the " Beacon". Affiliations: Inter'l. Institute of Political & Social Science. Club: Spartan, Olympic. Recreation: Cricket, gardening.Died 28, November 1971. Declared National Hero 28th April1998.

The Honourable Dr. Hugh Gordon Hylvester Cummings, M.D., C.M., C.B.E. Born St. James, February 02, 1891, son of Williams Payne Cummings and his wife, Dulceina nee Hutson, Educated Welches Combined Sch.; Combermere Sch.;

Harrison College; Queen's Univ. (Ontario). Religion: Anglican. Married Nov., 1920, Gladys Sybil Morrison: 3 sons, 2 daughters. Career: Deputy Premier 1954 - 1958; Premier of Barbados 1958 - 1961. Minister of Social Services,, represented Barbados on several delegations to the U.K. and other Caribbean countries dealing with matters of trade, the sugar industry, commerce, labour recruitment, etc. Interests: Fraternal - Br. Order of Ancient Free Gardeners, Independent United Order of Mechanics, Odd Fellow. Club: Empire. Recreation: Tennis, swimming, cricket. Died 1967. Regarded as "Father of Local Government and Labour Relations Reform."

Prime Ministers

The Right Excellent Errol Walton Barrow, B.Sc., P. C., M.P., Prime Minister (1966 - 1976 & May 1986 - June 1987), Minister of Finance and of External Affairs; barrister. Born St. Lucy, Jan. 21, 1920, son of Rev. Reginald Grant Barrow and late Ruth nee O'Neal his wife (sister of Dr. C.D O'Neal, M.H.A., founder of Democratic League). Educated Wesley Hall, Combermere, Harrison College; London Univ. (B.Sc., LLB. 1948, Econ., 1950). Married Nov. 18, 1945, Carolyn, daughter of Rev. Dr. George M. Plaskett, S.T.D., and Mrs. Plaskett: 1 son (David), 1 daughter. (Lesley). Career: R.A.F., World War II (Personal Navigation Officer to C.-in-C., Brit. Army of the Rhine, in 49

"On two occasions we have elected governments that appeared excessively strong, but in neither instance did the fears that a dictatorship would emerge materialise."

political landscape and the events of the 1930s could be considered the first political watershed of the century. During this era, we saw a regional phenomenon that started to **challenge colonialism** and ironically was linked to the exposure of several of our sons to the First World War. Hence we had the riots and several years later the British were forced to take note of the serious problems existing in this and other colonies.

By this time, increased exposure to socialism and democracy globally made it inevitable that **independence** would be placed on the Caribbean agenda. Of course, at the time independence was not seen as feasible for any Caribbean country, hence the **West Indies Federation** emerged as a convenient 'half-way house'. The political significance of this era lies in the advance of democracy through the extension of the franchise and the decline of colonialism. Cumulatively, these two events served to 'popularise' the politics of the century and ensure that hereditary or monarchical rule was irrevocably replaced by rule by the people, or popular government.

The ending of the federation ushered in the independence era, which for most Barbadians is still the most significant political achievement of the 20th century. In retrospect, independence can be considered a bittersweet achievement for the Caribbean, since it appears to be preventing us from moving to the regional level, which has the potential to offer us more security in this century.

It is the nonetheless fortunate that Barbados can boast that independence has ushered in a series of responsible governments and assisted in national development for the most part. We have been spared any serious political or electoral corruption that independence has facilitated in so many of our neighbouring territories.

Arguably the political low point for Barbados came in 1994, during the tenure of **Prime Minister Erskine Sandiford**, when our system of Parliamentary democracy was tested in a way that we have not experienced before or since. This was the point at which the Parliament of Barbados was asked for the first time in our history to examine the actions of a Prime Minister and express their confidence, or lack thereof, in the holder of this office. In the wake of this scenario, Parliament did express a lack of confidence in the PM and he thereafter decided to call an election, which the DLP lost. This high political drama camouflaged the significance of an event that brought a major political crisis to a close and conveyed power to a new administration, thereby demonstrating the resilience of democracy in Barbados and the political maturity of its people.

In the time since Independence until 2006, Barbados had held **eight general elections** and changed governments on three occasions and overtly amended the constitution once. We have retained the Westminster system with very few modifications. On two occasions we have elected governments that appeared excessively strong, but in neither instance did the fears that a dictatorship would emerge materialise.

operations with 2nd Tactical Air Force, invasion of Europe, on anti-submarine patrols, W. Atlantic), 1940-47; Island Scholar; M.P 1951 - 56, 1958 - 87., joined Democratic Labour Party, 1955; Chairman. D.L.P., 1960; Premier 1961 - 1966, Prime Minister, 1966 - 1976, 1986-1987. "Father of Independence". Affiliation: Freeman of Guild of Air Pilots & Navigators. Club: B'dos. Light Aeroplane, cruising. Recreations: Flying, Fishing, sailing, swimming, skin-diving, fishing, tennis, photography, cooking. Died: 1st June 1987: Named National Hero 1998.

The Right Honourable John Michael Geoffrey, Manningham Tom Adams, (M.A. (Oxon.) 1957, M.P (1967); barrister-at-law. Born Barbados, September. 24, 1931,

son of Sir Grantley Adams, C.M.G., Q.C., LL.B., etc. and his wife, Grace Thorne. Educated Harrison College, Barbados; Magdalen College, Oxford; Gray's Inn (1959). Career: B.B.C & ITV freelance broadcaster and producer 1955-62; President Barbados Labour Party 1971 - 1985. Leader of the BLP 1972 - 1985; MP 1966 - 1985; Leader of Opposition 1971 - 1976. Prime Minister of Barbados September 1976 - 11th March 1985. Second Prime Minister of Barbados. Married Genevieve Turner, June 2, 1962; father-in-law Philip Turner, Esq., L.L.B., etc. Two sons. Religion: Anglican. Interests: Gardening, watching and reading about cricket, philately. Died 11th March 1985. Regarded as the "Creator of Central Bank and the Airport to West Coast Highway." Creator of the Freehold Tenantry Purchase Act of 1981.

The Right Honourable Sir Harold Bernard St John, M.P., LL.B, Q.C. legislator, Barrister-in-Law; Pres. B'dos Law Society. Born: Aug. 16, 1931, Christ Church, son of the late Albert St. John & Mrs. J.B. Deane. Educated at Boys' Foundation: Harrsion College; London University, called to the Bar, Inner Temple 1954. Married Oct. 23, 1957, Stella Hope: 3 children. Political Career: MP for Christ Church 1966 - 1971, 1976 - 1986, 1991 - 2003 Leader of Opposition

1970 - 1976, Senator 1971- 1976, 1986 - 1991. Deputy Prime Minister 1976 - 1985; Prime Minister 11th March 1985 to 26 May 1985. Minister of International Trade. Knighted 1999. Died 2005. Regarded as Barbados' greatest Foreign Trade Negotiator and Internationally-respected expert on The Law of The Sea.

Sir Lloyd Erskine Sandiford, M.A., Born St. James, Barbados, March 24, 1937. Educated Coleridge Parry School, Harrison College, U.C.W.I. (now U.W.I), Jamaica, 1957-60

(B.A., Hons., English); Manchester University Eng,. 1961 - 63, M.A. (Econ.) 1963. Married Angelita Ricketts (Ph.D). Three children: two girls, one boy .Career: Barbados Scholar, 1956; Master, Kingston Coll., Jamaica, 1960 -61, and Harrison Coll., B'dos 1963-66; part-time Tutor & Lecturer, U.W.I.,

B'dos, 1963 - 65; Personal Adviser to Premier, Sept. 1966- Aug. 1967; Secy DLP., 1967; Senator 1967 - 1971; MP 1971 - 1999; Min. of Ed., 1967 - 1975;Minister of Health 1975 - 1976; Deputy PM 1986 -1987; Prime Minister June 1987 - September 1994; Distinguished Fellow SALISES 1994 - 2001; Tutor BCC 1977 - present. Hon LL.D (BCC) 2004. Address: Porters, St. James, Barbados. Knighted 2002. Noted for Revolutionary Educational Reform- "Father of the "Barbados Community College" and Creator of the Sherbourne Conference Centre.

The Right Hon. Owen Seymour Arthur, (BA, (UWI) 1971, 1973 Privy Councillor; Economist. Born Barbados Oct 17, 1949. Son of Frank Arthur, shop-keeper and his wife Iretha.

Educated at Coleridge-Parry, Harrison College, UWI Cave Hill 1968 - 1971 and Mona Campuses 1971 -73. Married twice. One daughter. Career: research Assistant 1973 -1974. I.S.E.R (Mona); 1974 - 1979 Assistant to the Chief Planner, National Planning Agency, 1979 - 81,

Director of Economics at the Jamaica Bauxite Institute. Chief Project Analyst, Ministry of Finance 1986: Chairman Barbados Agricultural Development Corporation. Director, Barbados Central Bank, Advisor to NHC. Political Career: Senator 1983 - 84; Member of Parliament for St. Peter 1984 - present; Leader of Opposition 1993 - 1994; Prime Minister 1994 to present; Minister of Finance and Minister of Culture; Chairman CARICOM Heads of Government; Honoured with several distinguished Awards since 1994. Regarded as "Founding Father of Caribbean Single Market and Economy" and Stalwart of the Regional Integration Movement.

/ Trevor G. Marshall

At the international level, Barbados has never assumed a controversial posture. We have continued to be active members of the **United Nations** and in 1994 hosted the UN Global Conference on Sustainable Development for Small Island Developing States. Unlike Caribbean countries like Jamaica, Barbados has never been associated with 'left-leaning' countries in the United Nations family and has been able to benefit comfortably from associations with countries on both sides of the ideological divide that existed before the end of the Cold War.

As globalisation continues to manifest itself and the full impact is realised, Barbados is discovering a new potential threat to democracy, which reduces the election exercise to one of semantics. The appropriate response to globalisation needs to be a regional one, which ironically could return Barbados to a mid-19th century form of governance. On this occasion, however, this form of governance would become not an end in itself, but a platform that provides access to South-South relations, which will open us to an entirely new set of global partners for our future development, which could be exciting. Alternatively we can try to persist as a nation state in the original conception and find ourselves once more as part of a colonial arrangement, supervised by the IMF or World Bank.

/ *Peter Wickham*

Willie Alleyne

The Economy
of Barbados

BARBADOS is, first and foremost, a developing country and historically its economy has been based on the traditional practice of cultivating the sugar cane crop and its principal products (sugar, molasses and rum) over a period of 350 years. However, the story of the last 50 years, since **Hurricane Janet** in 1955, has been one of steady and sometimes spectacular growth in several other areas, as the Barbadian economy has become one of the success stories of independence among former British Colonies.

Indeed the Barbados programme of **diversifying** away from sugar cane and agriculture generally and anchoring its economic development in tourism, manufacturing, informatics, offshore banking, foreign investment and related services is so successful that analysts are now talking about 'The Barbados Model'. We remember that 50 years ago Puerto Rico was identified as the developing country with the greatest potential for economic growth and development, based on foreign investment in its industries. Now as the 21st century nears the end of its first decade, the government is fully in control of the economy and Barbados is on course to become a First World economy by the year 2020.

This is no pipe dream as the Governor of the Central Bank, **Dr Marion Williams** emphasizes in her frequent analyses of the economy. Investor confidence is high says Dr Williams, and all sectors of the economy are contributing satisfactorily to the overall growth of this small country. Barbados' development strategy since the 1980s has been to consolidate its sugar base, but at the same time to pursue a mixed economy.

Barbados experienced steady economic development and diversification following World War II, in many ways outperforming all the Leeward and

> *"Now as the 21st century nears the end of its first decade, the government is fully in control of the economy and Barbados is on course to become a First World economy by the year 2020."*

above / the 'Dover Court' Office of Tower Bucknall Austin. Operating in Barbados and the Eastern Caribbean since 1993, Tower Bucknall Austin, has developed a reputation for high quality specialised service within the construction and property arenas. They aim to be the leading professional construction and property consultancy services provider in Barbados and the Caribbean by blending human and technological resources and tailoring their services to meet the specific requirements of their clients. They are committed to ensuring that projects are seen through seamlessly from concept to completion

top / currently, the Barbados Public Workers' Co-operative Credit Union Ltd has two locations: the head office (pictured) situated at Olive Trotman House in St Michael and its branch office located on Broad Street, Bridgetown

left / the Sol Group is the Caribbean's largest independent oil company, having acquired Shell's fuel businesses in 10 countries in the Eastern Caribbean, Guyana, Suriname and Belize in February 2005 and the further Shell retail businesses in Puerto Rico in August 2006. Sol operates 288 Shell-branded retail stations, as well as commercial, lubricants, aviation refuelling, marine and LPG businesses. Sol has a regional focus that is unique. In order to be a highly responsive customer-centred organisation, the company is run by local offices that can make key decisions

Windward Islands. The economy was transformed from one dependent on agriculture, primarily sugar, for a third of its **gross domestic product** (GDP) to one considered relatively diversified with the development of tourism and manufacturing sectors. By 1980 agriculture accounted for a mere 9 per cent of GDP, whereas the wholesale and retail trade had grown to about 17 per cent, general services to 14 per cent, manufacturing to 12 per cent and government services and tourism to 11 per cent each. At the same time, the **standard of living** had increased remarkably as the nation elevated itself from the ranks of low-income countries to those of middle-income countries.

Barbados' economic success could be linked to many factors. The island had long been a model of social and political stability that helped to attract both public and private foreign investment. The government also assisted with the infrastructural development required of an expanding economy, including a sound educational system. Since the 1970s successive administrations have made it their first priority not to permit the economy to fall into the same economic problems as has beset Jamaica and Guyana. The government arranged loans with carefully-selected partners but did not indulge in excess borrowing.

Since the 1980s when Barbados underwent a surveillance programme by the **International Monetary Fund**, the island has pursued a policy of **fiscal prudence** so that the economy would not be confronted with the crisis of devaluation. The 8 per cent cut in government workers' salaries of 1991 worked effectively to dampen excess debt and has proved to be an incentive to the Arthur administration, which has been in office since 1994, to take creative measures to avoid the need to borrow from the IMF and thus incur the rigid conditionalities that are an integral part of World Bank and IMF packages.

Barbados has long boasted an excellent education system, which features compulsory free school attendance until the age 16, the point at which young people can enter the work force. The effect of this is that every year the economy absorbs a fresh stock of well-educated, trainable young people. With a literacy rate of some 98 per cent the island has directed its young people towards the service industries, self-employment, entrepreneurship and investment in neighbouring CARICOM countries.

With an unemployment rate of 9.3 per cent, (the lowest in the region) Barbados is creating a new model of Caribbean efficiency and economic growth. Every sector of the economy is growing at a rate of at least 2.5 per cent and with the promise of an eminently trainable workforce, the overall economic prospects look good.

The traditional **agriculture sector** is perhaps the least well endowed as sugar cane production is concentrated on less than 35,000 hectares now but, as Minister of Agriculture, Erskine Griffith assures Barbadians, this sugar sector will soon be redirected towards producing ethanol and other biodiversity products, which will help Barbados reduce its energy bill and its dependence on oil for fuel.

The sector that leads the way in Barbados and provides the multiplier for the economy is undoubtedly **tourism**, both the land-based, hotel-oriented type and

"With an unemployment rate of 9.3 per cent, (the lowest in the region) Barbados is creating a new model of Caribbean efficiency and economic growth."

above / the elegant Mahogany Bay Townhouses, Saint James, designed by Gillespie & Steel Associates – a Barbadian company offering architectural, planning, and project management services in the Eastern Caribbean. Established in 1969 the firm has gained immeasurable experience in a wide range of projects having been active in the industry for nearly 40 years.

top / established in 1888, Collins Limited is one of the leading distributors of prescription and OTC pharmaceuticals, hospital supplies and toiletries in the Caribbean. They are also major distributors of nutritionals, confectionery, canned fruit and juices and operate one of the largest retail pharmacies in the region

left / Abacus Builders Inc has been 'creating lifestyles' for homeowners in Barbados for the past 12 years. Producing high quality, competitively priced homes in some of the most prestigious developments on the island, their team of knowledgeable and friendly staff will make it easy for you to create your lifestyle.

opposite top / Bridgetown Port

opposite bottom / New Bridgetown

above / a privately-owned company headquartered in Barbados, Interamericana Trading Corporation (ITC) is one of the leading automobile distributors in the Caribbean and Latin America, with a network of over 100 dealers in 32 countries. The company is the region's official representative for some of the world's leading manufacturers including Daimler Chrysler, Suzuki and Porsche

top / for over 95 years the Royal Bank of Canada has served clients in Barbados, helping generations of families meet their personal and business banking needs. Their knowledgeable team of employees focuses on getting to know their clients, offering them a full range of products and services to help achieve their financial goals

left / at Scotiabank, Corporate Social Responsibility is an integral part of how they do business, affording them the opportunity to make a difference to their customers, their employees, the environment and the communities they serve. Their involvement is focused on culture, education, sports and health matters, with special emphasis on youth

the cruise-ship variety. Barbados is working hard to expand its hotel space and to boost the growth in villas, guesthouses and motels. With expansion to the airport and the upgrading of all its ancillary services the island's lone airport now clears some 450,000 tourists per annum. Today Barbados is rated the best tourism-oriented country in the world.

The Bridgetown port provides berth for some eight mega-cruise ships with up to 9.6 metre draughts. The port has a very modern cruise terminal offering 30,000 square feet of space for ultra-modern duty-free shops, providing a wide variety of local and overseas goods. Together with the airport, the harbour now admits over a million tourists onto the island every year. Barbados has confounded all those critics who have argued that tourism is a fragile base on which to develop a thriving, prosperous economy. Its track record, since 1957 when the **Hotel Aids Act** was passed and the Tourist Board came into existence, is so strong that observers are speaking of the '**Barbados miracle**'.

There is an entire array of traditional services within the industry and 'new' ones such as sports tourism, education tourism and heritage tourism, which are all contributing to the economic growth of the island.

The newest sector is that of '**cultural industries**' that combine the best of the tourism-based activities with the explosive arts of music, dance and drama, mixed with arts and crafts, film, video and photography to establish a new and excitingly viable arena for residents to explore. Thus Crop Over, the island's premier folk festival, and its six other festivals now contribute handsomely to GNP.

Within the traditional sector, **banking** has emerged as a strong leader, with the banks – traditionally cautious and conservative in their policies – now operating like credit unions, lending for a variety of consumer items, as well as for land purchase and development projects, which contain several risks. The Barbados National Bank, now owned by Trinidad and Tobago, is a strong leader in this field and is supporting the economic development drive in a spectacular manner.

Consumers now have more reason to feel confident in the Barbados economy. There is the consumer **Guarantee Act** of 2002, which has narrowed the boundary between the buyers and the sellers and, although there is no private consumer body, it can be said that the average citizen is protected from exploitation.

Finally, there is an improvement in the **technology** available, which has improved the society beyond the imagination of our grandparents. Barbados has total coverage of electricity, telephones, both mobile and land-based, and there are laser, optics and microchip systems all through the society. Communication is now at First World level and manufacturing is expanding. The Barbados economy is now far more than sugar and tourism, and provided we can solve our transportation problems (small roads, too many vehicles, gridlock and pollution), it could well be on its way to becoming a high middle-ranking economic force in just over a decade's time.

/ Ronnie McD Squires

> *"Today Barbados is rated the best tourism-oriented country in the world."*

Chickmont Foods Ltd are an amalgamation of three poultry companies located in a custom built plant off the ABC Highway, located in the south of the island. They holds the distinction of being the only ISO 9001 and HACCP certified processing plant in Barbados. This achievement attests to their first-class nature of our facilities and organization.

above / GAS Security Services (Barbados) Ltd is part of Group 4 Securicor and is a market leader in providing security services, security systems and cash services. G4S is one of the world's largest security solutions groups, operating in over 100 countries with over 500 employees in Barbados

top / Lasco (Barbados) Limited was established in 1989 and are the distributors of pharmaceuticals, hair-care products and the Lasco Food Drink range of products. The company represents international pharmaceutical brands including Schering AG, Roche and BSN Medical. The distribution of Soft Sheen Carson, Organics Roots, Avon and Ontex also form part of their portfolio. Catering to the needs of their customers is paramount, as they strive to deliver 'Quality Service Every Time'

left / an employee at Atlantis Sea Food Inc cuts fish in preparation for packaging. Atlantis Sea Food carry a wide selection of frozen and fresh fish and seafood, ranging from shellfish to flying fish. Fish Fyne, their brand of frozen fish like dolphin (mahi mahi), bangamary and the Barbadian favourite catch, flying fish, are vacuum-sealed and are available for export. If you are visiting Barbados, be sure to check the local supermarkets and mini-marts for their brand

Investment Challenges – Past & Present

above / located in the fast-growing Warrens business district, ABS is a company offering cutting-edge electronic solutions and services to today's demanding market-place. They deliver high-quality photo-ID solutions and card production services, point-of-sale solutions, access control, monitoring and security systems all backed by trained support personnel

top / Barbados Institute of Management and Productivity (BIMAP) was established in 1971 by the joint efforts of government and private sector to improve the efficiency and effectiveness of management and to increase national productivity. BIMAP offers a comprehensive range of services in the areas of management training, consulting, research and small business development to its members and clients. Courses for the award of a certificate, a diploma and a degree are offered. The MSc and MBA programmes are conducted in collaboration with the University of Surrey, U.K. The Institute has modern facilities, computer laboratories and equipment to facilitate the delivery of its programmes and services at its Wildey HQ and also at its Bridgetown office

NO SCRIPT on investments in Barbados would be complete without specifying that the country's social past has, in no small measure, characterised the present attitude towards investment and further, promises to be a barometer for future investment policy.

Indeed, it is no unfounded premise that in every country there is a particular date and time in history that is a constant reminder of an event that has lead to a major transformation in the livelihood of its citizens. For Barbados, it is the 1937 protests for national recognition and economic betterment that will forever be etched in the social prologue of the island, not so much from the extent of what occurred on the date in question, but more so from the reports and recommendations from those who were charged with this responsibility.

The 1943 Dean Commission established by then Governor Sir Grattan Bushe emphasised the need for **reformation in land ownership**. Land and house ownership is, for many, the most prized investment. However, this call for reformation was heeded only with the 1980 passage of the **Tenantries (Freehold Purchase) Act**, whereby those who laboured in the foundation of Independence were allowed to acquire their house spots at the concessionary rate of 10 cents per square foot. Some 40 years before the passage of this progressive legislation, an opportunity was provided for ordinary Barbadians to invest in the banking industry, which was foreign dominated. It was in 1938 that Fredrick D McDonald Symmonds established the **Barbados Cooperative Bank** with prospective investors being encouraged to acquire shares on a piecemeal basis. This institution only succeeded in enlisting the hostility of the establishment and the subsequent estrangement of the very masses for whom he was fending.

above / KPMG Barbados is a member firm of KPMG Caricom, the regional governance entity comprising the KPMG member firms in Barbados, the Eastern Caribbean, Jamaica and Trinidad and Tobago. KPMG leverages the combined skills, knowledge and experience of their partners and staff to offer coordinated audit, tax and advisory services in Barbados and across the region

top / Island Gold Realty and Fairways Real Estate specialise in townhouse and apartment complexes. They are the management agents for Rockley Golf and Country Club, El Sol Sureno, Durants, The Barbados Golf Club and Gunsite (pictured). As well as dealing with both long and short-term rentals, they also offer a broad spectrum of management and sales expertise

left / WAMCO Data Management is the largest local provider of data network services, connecting Barbados to the world of international business. Using robust, state-of-the-art network technologies, the company offers wide area network connectivity, high-speed internet access and web-related services, co-location and data storage solutions to clients in all sectors of the Barbados business community

However, 31 years later, another experiment in mass **exposure to investment** through **share ownership** was engineered by D A L 'Tony' Pile, a distinguished Attorney-at-Law. On April 25, 1969, Mr Pile established the **Barbados Unit Trust** in an effort to bridge the vacuum of opportunity for small investors to participate in both local and foreign investments.

The fund did not benefit from any Government tax incentive and, therefore, unlike the other Mutual Funds that followed some years afterwards, its growth was stymied. Despite the absence of any tax incentives, the Unit Trust proved attractive to local investors and at the time of its last distribution on December 15, 1985 there were 619,244 unit holders. Following the termination of the Unit Trust in 1986, 11 Mutual Funds have been incorporated. With the specific help of an annual $10,000 tax allowance, these Funds have grown significantly in number as well as portfolio size providing investment opportunities to nationals both resident and abroad.

In small developing countries, the need to provide direct measures to give ordinary citizens a stake in ownership of productive assets becomes a more urgent priority.

As if responding to the clarion call of the working class, Prime Minister, 'Tom' Adams, in his 1979 Financial Statement and Budgetary Proposals affirmed that his Government would give full support to **the establishment of a Stock Market** for the free trading in securities and shares in public companies. The principal objectives of this initiative were cited as the encouragement of major private companies to become public, the provision of direct opportunity for personal investment in productive activity through share ownership and the creation of a wider ownership of shares.

Provision was also made for a bonus-share scheme that, for the first time, provided workers with a tax incentive scheme, which allowed for active participation in ownership of shares in their work place. Additionally, provision was made for a tax exemption of shares issued in lieu of retirement gifts up to the value of $5,000 along with an income tax concession of $10,000 on all 'new' shares acquired.

The passage of the **Securities Exchange Act 1982** brought reality of purpose to the proposals outlined by Tom Adams in his 1979 Budget. Over time it seemed inevitable that the three exchanges in Barbados, Trinidad and Tobago and Jamaica would seek to proceed on a common front. Therefore, it came as no surprise when, at their 10th Ministerial meeting in Grenada in 1989, the heads of CARICOM Government, through the **Grand Anse Declaration**, resolved that 'a scheme for movement of capital should be introduced by 1993 with cross listing and trading of securities on existing stock exchanges'. Like any other investment activity, the process of cross listing has had its peaks and valleys but, generally, an acceptable standard of regional understanding and cooperation appears to have been maintained throughout. However, the reality of a Caribbean Stock Exchange still seems far off.

above / Island Heritage is a regional property insurer that is domiciled in Grand Cayman. The company was established in 1996 out of the recognition that a new type of insurance company was needed for the Caribbean. Through its branch office in Barbados and agency networks in several other islands in the region, it is poised to service the needs of the Caribbean property owner

"Prime Minister, 'Tom' Adams, in his 1979 Financial Statement and Budgetary Proposals affirmed that his Government would give full support to the establishment of a Stock Market."

In today's globalized market and economy, there are no longer any barriers to prevent or limit **foreign portfolio investment**. In times past, such activities took second place to direct foreign investment, which was encouraged through the provision of fiscal and other incentives.

Today's global environment calls for fresh thinking on the role and conditions for more foreign portfolio investment by business corporations, particularly in areas of job creation and foreign-exchange generation through export industries. Like most developing countries, the principal advantage of foreign portfolio equity investment is that it opens the possibility of introducing a vast new source of equity capital inflow without any substantial lost of domestic control. Moreover, enhanced portfolio investment can bolster the capital bases of corporations and, where they exist, alleviate high corporate debt/equity ratios.

Therefore, the philosophy of investment in Barbados can best be characterised as a deliberately-intended drive towards a social market economy. Consequently, Government policy is geared towards promoting a progressive and prosperous social economy by insisting on a more widely-dispersed ownership of property and assets. In this way, the benefits and degree of personal independence that result from ownership and investment become widely available instead of being confined to the few.

/ Hilford Murrell

above / the Barbados Coalition of Service Industries Inc has benefited many businesses in this sector, which it has helped to develop and diversify.

below / since 1988 Ocean Fisheries have been processing and sourcing, both locally and internationally, a wide range of fine seafood for the local market to best meet the needs and standards of their customers. They are respected as the leading supplier of fresh and frozen fish and seafood in the industry

opposite top / J E Security Systems & Services Inc is a Barbados-based security provider specialising in the design, installation and service of security equipment for residential, commercial and industrial markets since 1992. They offer comprehensive solutions to any security situation and their personalised approach and dedication to customer satisfaction allows the company to know their customers by name

opposite bottom / the head office of the British American Insurance Company Ltd. Theirs is a story of commitment, community and integrity. The cornerstone of Caribbean growth and development has been solid democracies and strong and trusted financial institutions. For over 45 years, British American Insurance has not been simply a bystander in the Caribbean story, but a participant – shapers of a proud past and a promising future

above / the HQ of Sagicor Financial Corporation, the Sagicor Corporate Centre. Sagicor is synonymous with world-class financial services in the Caribbean. This dynamic, indigenous company, with a proud history dating back to 1840, offers a wide range of financial services, including life and health insurance, annuities, pensions, property and casualty insurance, banking, as well as investment services. Operating in 20 countries throughout the Caribbean, the US and Latin America, Sagicor has developed an incomparable reputation because of its financial stability

left / established in 1901, BICO Ltd is the premier ice-cream maker in the Caribbean, with exports throughout the region from Guyana to Belize. In addition the company operates a huge commercial chilled and frozen storage facility at the Bridgetown Harbour

The Barbados Stock Exchange

THE **Barbados Stock Exchange** (BSE), formerly the Securities Exchange of Barbados, was re-incorporated on August 2, 2001 with the passage of the **Securities Act 2001-13**, which also enabled the establishment of the Barbados **Securities Commission**. The Commission is responsible for the regulation of the Barbados Capital Market, including all public companies whether listed or not.

The Barbados Stock Exchange and its wholly-owned subsidiary, the **Barbados Central Securities Depository** (BCSDI) are designated as **Self-Regulatory Organisations** (SROs) under the Securities Act 2001-13, but also are regulated in turn by the Securities Commission.

The BSE is an association of Member-Brokers, operating a central marketplace for trading Securities.

The original trading facility, the Securities Exchange of Barbados, was established in 1987 under the Securities Exchange Act, Cap 318A, of 1982. The Securities Act 2001-13 repealed and replaced the original Act of 1982. However the BSE remains a privately owned (by its Members), non-profit, organisation.

A **Board of Directors** through a General Manager administers the affairs of the BSE. The Board of the BSE consists of four designated members, four elected and one independent. The four designated members represent the Central Bank of Barbados, the Bar Association, the Barbados Chamber of Commerce and Industry and the Institute of Bankers. The elected members are chosen from the Membership of the Stock Exchange.

The Board of Directors sets By-Laws and Rules to regulate the affairs and business of the Exchange. Included in the By-Laws and Rules are standards and

above / the main offices of the Barbados Shipping & Trading (BS&T) Company Ltd, which is a leading and diversified public company in the Barbadian community. It has some 25 companies, many of which are market leaders in their respective sectors. Listed on the Barbados Stock Exchange and the Trinidad & Tobago Stock Exchange, BS&T also has 13 associated company investments, notably Banks Holdings, Almond Resorts and Gablewoods Supermart

left / managers and staff at the Broad Street location of RBTT Bank Barbados Limited (formerly Caribbean Commercial Bank). A wholly-owned subsidiary of RBTT Financial Holdings Limited, it was acquired on June 24, 2004. With four branches operating in Barbados, the bank offers a full range of innovative financial products and services catering to the needs of its individual and commercial customers, as well as its public and private sector clients

rules of conduct to which members must adhere. Only **Registered Brokers**, representing Members of the BSE are allowed to trade securities on the Exchange.

Currently, there are 26 listed companies on the Board of the BSE including six cross-listed companies from within CARICOM but outside of Barbados.

The **Market Capitalisation** at December 31, 2001 was $3,656,210,138.98 for the Local Market, $2,755,405,123.75 for the Cross-Listed Market and $22,833,000.20 for the Junior Market. The BSE Local index at the same point was 2,107.29. When you compare that to our performance at December 31, 2005 it can be seen that the market has grown considerably; Market Capitalisation was $10,970,643,855.10 for the Local Market, an increase of 200.06 per cent, and $11,814,250,846.13 for the Cross-Listed market, an increase of 328.77 per cent. The BSE Local Index at December 31, 2005 was 3,927.58, an increase of 86.38 per cent; and the Cross-Listed Index moved from 901.25 to 2,230.34 – an increase of 155.08 per cent.

The Trade System

Only Members or their authorised Brokers may trade on the Exchange. A Broker may trade for his own account, where he acts as principal, or a member may become an agent and trade on behalf of a client.

On July 4, 2001, the Exchange switched from the manual, open auction outcry method of trading, to electronic, trading using the Order-routing method. Orders/calls may be given at specific prices within a 10 per cent limit above or below the previous closing price. Orders are queued immediately but trades occur only when two or more orders match. Limit orders at specified prices are executed at that price or better and it is the responsibility of the Brokers to ensure that clients settle their accounts/trades within the specified time of T + 5, or five business days after trade day. Effective January 1, 2006, this settlement cycle was reduced to T + 3.

Barbados Central Securities Depository Inc (BCSDI)

The BCSDI is a wholly owned Subsidiary of the Barbados Stock Exchange. It is a facility for holding securities and enables share transactions to be processed by book entry. A Book-Entry System facilitates the change of ownership of Securities electronically, without the need for the movement of physical documents (i.e. the BCSDI is an electronic means of recording the ownership of shares).

The BCSDI registers the stock in the name of the beneficial owner. The certificates are held physically in their vault. The BCSDI also records the securities movements in the name of the beneficial owner using the National Identification Number. The BCSDI's book-entry system has shortened the settlement cycle and ensures that investors receive payment for shares sold and ownership of shares purchased within a shorter time.

Barbados Tourism Investment Inc (BTI) was formed under the Companies Act in 1998 by the Government of Barbados to facilitate investment in the vital tourism sector. BTI has been successful in carrying out its mandate through its ongoing work, developing a portfolio of tourism-related properties, managing the implementation of the Urban Rehabilitation Programme in the main tourism centres and facilitating both public and private sector-owned investment in the tourism and hospitality sector in Barbados. Over the next five years BTI will participate with private sector investors in a number of projects, including a major upscale resort, a marina and a mixed-use commercial development in Bridgetown.

above / Goddard Enterprises Ltd. (GEL) is a Barbadian-based multi-national organisation operating in 22 countries through fifty-eight (58) subsidiaries and associated companies, with a staff compliment of over 3,200. Its operations include manufacturing, catering, trading, general insurance, financial and other services and investment holdings. The Group has net assets of over BDS $400 million and turnover of over BDS $650 million. Picture shows managers and staff preparing meals for the next flight

left / Cable & Wireless is the only full service telecommunications provider in Barbados, offering fixed line, broadband and mobile services to their corporate and residential customers, as well as business system solutions. With over 120 years of service to Barbados they have continued to offer cutting edge technology through continued investment, provide superior network coverage and deliver the best value

Listing Requirements

A company wishing to list on the Exchange must apply for a Listing and must meet the following basic criteria before the listing is approved:

- The Company must be registered and in good standing with the Registrar of Companies
- Be a profit-making venture with minimum assets of one million dollars
- Demonstrate adequate working capital (based on the previous three years financials and three years projections)
- Evidence of competent management
- Have a positive dividend profile over the three preceding years

After approval by the Barbados Stock Exchange, Listed Companies, including Officers and Directors, must observe and comply with the Rules and By-Laws of the Exchange and are required to meet on-going requirements outlined in the Listing Agreement as well. These include requirements for disclosures of the interim and audited Financial Statements as well as any material changes affecting the affairs, business, operations or capital structure of the company which could in any way affect the shareholders.

Junior Market

The Junior Market commenced operation in October 1999 and its intention is to cater to those smaller or newer public companies, which may not meet all the necessary requirements for listing in the Regular Market, such as financial requirements and history. There ongoing listing requirements of providing financial information as well as information on any material changes in the organisation, must be provided in a similar way to that required by companies listed on the Regular Market.

Chairpersons and General Managers

Over the years the Barbados Stock Exchange and its forerunner the Securities Exchange of Barbados has been served with some outstanding Chairpersons. The first was Mr Colin Goddard, who served from June 1, 1987 to December 17, 1997. Mr Shastrie Ablack, who served from December 17, 1997 to November 1998, followed him. The Third Chair was Mr Neville Smith, who served from June 18, 1999 to May 4, 2000. He was followed by Dr Patricia Downes-Grant (July 14, 2000 until November 23, 2004), while the current Chair of the Exchange is Mr Andrew St John, who took over on November 23, 2004.

The Exchange has been served ably by its three General Managers and one Acting General Manager over is 18-year history. They were Mr Anthony Johnson, who was General Manager from February 1, 1986 to June 30, 1994. He was responsible for the setting up the Securities Exchange of Barbados and he saw the first trades occur on June 12, 1987. Mrs Virginia Mapp, who served from September 1, 1994 to December 31, 2002, followed him. She was

> "In small developing countries, the need to provide direct measures to give ordinary citizens a stake in ownership of productive assets becomes a more urgent priority."

above / the Checker Hall, St Lucy, site of the Arawak Cement Company Limited. A subsidiary of the TCL Group, the company has been producing a consistently high quality of Portland cement – using 98 per cent of Barbadian raw materials – since 1984. Arawak is at the forefront of the industrial sector of the Barbados economy. It has been recognised as a model for how to turn around what was considered a problematic industrial plant. All employees are given the opportunity to excel in their performance and endeavours. Arawak took the Barbados Industrial Development Corporation's Prestigious Pillar of Industry Award for 2003 and 2004, recognising the company as the leader in the manufacturing service sector

left / in 1978 Sunpower was founded by the company's mechanical engineer, and produced by a handful of skilled craftsmen. They are now No1 in service-response, and are known for using quality materials that produce lasting solar systems. They are proud of their experienced service and installation teams that are capable of inspecting and servicing any brand

responsible for the transition of the Exchange from the Securities Exchange of Barbados to the Barbados Stock Exchange Inc on August 2, 2001, and also the move from an open out-cry method of trading to full electronic trading.

During 2003 (January 1 to October 31), Ms Tessa Pickering acted as General Manager. During this period she oversaw an important change within the electronic trading engine with the introduction of a tight-coupling system. The system of tight-coupling ensures that trades are transmitted as 'matched' transactions. This means that details of the trades from buyer and seller have already been matched (and verified) by the computer. The current General Manager of the Barbados Stock Exchange Inc is Marlon Yarde, who took up the position from November 1, 2003. He has the mandate of promoting the activities of the Exchange through education to foster an environment of confidence and trust in the activities of the capital markets, so that all Barbadians would participate in the trading of financial instruments.

The vision is simple, 'To be a vibrant and lasting Caribbean Institution by facilitating wealth creation through trading on an efficient and cost-effective Exchange', not only wanting 'To be a vibrant and lasting Caribbean Institution', but a 'great and lasting Caribbean Institution'.

The goal of the BSE is to allow participants to create wealth for themselves and to further engender confidence and trust in the market by letting people know what the Exchange is about and how it can assist them in achieving their financial objectives. The BSE is very passionate about its responsibilities.

/ *Marlon Yarde*

below / the main site of Williams Industries Inc, a 35-year-old Barbados-based Pan-Caribbean conglomerate with significant investments in several fields, including the manufacture of metal products, equipment rental, electrical contracting, real estate development, hardware and lumber distribution, warehousing, tourism, farming, well drilling, water desalination and sewage treatment

Willie Alleyne

La Barbade: Découvrez les Caraïbes dans toute leur splendeur

LA BARBADE. L'île des Caraïbes où se lève le soleil. La Barbade. Contrée des poissons volants argentés. La Barbade. En route pour une véritable aventure caribéenne. La Barbade.

Les Indiens Arawak habitèrent l'île pendant plus de 2000 ans avant de laisser la place aux Caribes. On a bien découvert des vestiges du séjour des Indiens à la Barbade, mais la raison et la manière dont ils ont quitté l'île restent un mystère. Lorsque les Portugais arrivèrent en 1536, ils avaient disparus sans laisser de traces.

Les Portugais quittèrent l'île à leur tour, et lorsqu'en 1625 les Anglais débarquèrent de leur navire *The Olive Blossom* dans une région portant à présent le nom de Holetown, ils la trouvèrent inhabitée et la déclarèrent territoire du roi d'Angleterre James. Quatre-vingt colons et 10 esclaves ne tardèrent pas à arriver le 17 février 1627, et contribuèrent à faire de cette île l'une des colonies les plus riches d'Angleterre.

Depuis le jour de l'indépendance, le 30 novembre 1966, jusqu'à ce jour, la Barbade n'a cessé d'évoluer pour devenir l'île la plus développée des Caraïbes et l'un des petits états insulaires les plus admirés au monde. Selon l'indice de développement humain de l'ONU, la Barbade, avec ses 430 kilomètres carré et ses quelques 270 000 habitants, fait également partie du peloton de tête des pays en voie de développement.

Dans ce pays divisé en 11 communes, les visiteurs remarquent très rapidement que la diversité du paysage est à vous couper le souffle. A l'ouest et au sud de l'île, les cocotiers bordent les plages de sable blanc s'élançant vers une mer

above / Mullin's Bay, Saint Peter

opposite / Bathsheba, Saint Joseph

above / Six Men's Bay, Saint Peter

top / Paynes Bay Beach, Saint James

calme bleu azur, tandis qu'au nord et à l'est, les falaises côtoient l'océan agité. Le paysage vallonné du Scotland District offre également un contraste agréable avec les plaines de l'ouest et du sud. Les deux gros pôles d'arrivée sur l'île sont Grantley Adams International Airport, à 18 km de la capitale Bridgetown, et le port de Bridgetown, à un peu plus d'un kilomètre du centre ville.

L'île offre des logements pour tous les goûts et budgets: des hôtels all-inclusive, des petits hôtels, des appartements en location, des chambres d'hôtes ou des villas. Ceux-ci sont tous supervisés par le *Quality Assurance Department of the Barbados Tourism Authority* (le département assurance qualité des autorités du tourisme à la Barbade). Ces hôtels et les nombreux restaurants offrent dans des cadres splendides des mets exquis, des spécialités locales ou de la cuisine internationale, toujours servis avec une touche caribéenne unique.

Bien entendu, le traditionnel "soleil, mer et plage" est offert à la Barbade, mais l'île propose également un autre classique: visites, shopping et sport. Les visites relèvent du pur bonheur : des tours en hélicoptère et vues aériennes magnifiques aux aventures sous-marines extraordinaires offertes par le sous-marin *Atlantis*. Sans compter la vue splendide de Cherry Tree Hill, le charme irrésistible de Sunbury et les ruines fascinantes de Farley Hill.

L'histoire militaire de la Barbade a laissé ses traces : le *Barbados Museum*, une ancienne prison militaire britannique, qui est devenue une collection de curiosités, certes modeste, mais très intéressante; la *Gun Hill Signal Station* et son magnifique lion taillé dans de la pierre de corail; la *Garrison Area*, riche en vestiges avec notamment la *Bush Hill House*, le seul endroit en dehors des Etats-Unis où George Washington a passé la nuit.

Les jardins botaniques de l'île, les *Andromeda Botanic Gardens*, la *Flower Forest* et l'*Orchid World*, abondent de fleurs exotiques, et les quelques 10 médailles d'or gagnées par l'association d'horticulture lors du prestigieux *Chelsea Flower Show* en Angleterre témoignent de la beauté et de la qualité des fleurs de la Barbade.

La réserve naturelle de *Graeme Hall Swamp*, refuge pour de nombreux oiseaux, pour la plupart migrateurs, et la *Barbados Wildlife Reserve*, vous garantissant pratiquement d'apercevoir les singes verts africains (le seul animal sauvage en abondance sur l'île) valent le détour. Les fans d'écotourisme peuvent faire une excursion agréable avec *Hike Barbados*.

La Barbade est le pays du rhum, et cet alcool est la raison d'être de diverses attractions: le Centre de Visite de *Mount Gay Rum*; la distillerie de rhum Foursquare et le Heritage Park; le *Malibu Visitors Centre*. Le punch, dont vous n'aurez jamais assez, est apparemment totalement inoffensif! N'oublions pas non plus la *Banks Breweries*, la demeure de la bière du pays, offrant également une visite très populaire.

Broad Street est la rue qu'il vous faut pour faire votre shopping hors taxes. Vous y trouverez les grandes marques de produits électroniques, d'ornements en verre et cristal, de porcelaine, d'appareils photo, de parfums et de spiritueux.

Vous pourrez également dégoter des vêtements haute couture dans les boutiques de la côte ouest et sud, où de nombreux créateurs barbadiens vous offriront sans aucun doute des créations des plus originales. Vous découvrirez également la touche barbadienne dans la poterie, vannerie, papeterie, peinture, l'art de travailler le fil de fer et les coquillages... Tout ça au *Pelican Village*, où tout produit est garanti "made in Barbados".

Le cricket, parmi tous les sports, est le chouchou dans ce coin des Caraïbes. Au fil des ans, l'île a produit quelques uns des meilleurs athlètes de ce sport, notamment le seul héro national en vie : Sir Garfield Sobers, reconnu comme étant le meilleur joueur de cricket de l'histoire. Mais, aujourd'hui, on lit le mot «golf» sur toutes les lèvres, même sur celles de Sir Garfield. Les golfeurs trouveront leur bonheur au célèbre *Royal Westmoreland Golf and Country Club* ainsi que sur le terrain invariablement parfait du *Sandy Lane Golf Club*. Le *Barbados Golf Club* à Durants dans le Christ Church vaut également le détour avec son parcours de championnat 18 trous.

Tennis, équitation, hockey, jogging, football, cyclisme, vol à voile, parachutisme ascensionnel, surf, planche à voile, ski nautique, jet ski, voile et pêche en haute mer ne sont que quelques-uns des sports terrestres et aquatiques offerts. La dernière mode est la nage, plus précisément la nage avec masque et tuba, avec les tortues, la saison des tortues luth étant mars/juillet et celle des tortues caret, avril/octobre.

Un tour sur le bateau pirate *Jolly Roger* ou sur le bateau *Harbour Master* vous garantit un moment de plaisir, tandis que des plus petits catamarans vous proposent un divertissement plus exclusif. Sur la terre ferme, l'île se réveille le soir après le dîner lors des spectacles tels que le "Bajan Roots and Rhythms" ou dans les boîtes de nuit comme After Dark, Harbour Lights et le Boatyard.

Les festivals divertissent les visiteurs tout au long de l'année, du *Barbados Jazz Festival* en janvier, affichant une excellente combinaison d'artistes du pays et d'artistes internationaux tels que Patti LaBelle, Alicia Keyes et Lionel Richie, au plus sophistiqué *Holders Season* en mars, offrant tout ce qu'il y a de mieux en matière d'opéra, Shakespeare et diverses formes d'art surprenantes.

Après ces heures d'ivresse, le soleil doit inévitablement se coucher. A ce moment-là, les chanceux apercevront les lumières vertes, rares, presque mythiques. Ceux qui ne les verront pas, n'en auront pas moins de chance : après tout, ils sont à la Barbade et rêvent d'y acheter une maison. Investir dans le paradis ? Pas une mauvaise idée du tout!

Barbados: Erleben Sie die Karibik

above & opposite / the Grand Kadooment, finale of the annual Crop Over festival

BARBADOS. Die Insel in der Karibik, an der die Sonne zuerst aufgeht. Barbados. Land der silbernen Fliegenden Fische. Barbados. Erleben Sie die wahre Karibik. Barbados.

Mehr als 2000 Jahre lang bewohnten die Arawak-Indianer die Insel, gefolgt von den Kariben. Reste ihres Aufenthaltes in Barbados wurden entdeckt, doch warum und wie sie die Insel verließen, bleibt weiterhin ein Rätsel. Als die Portugiesen 1536 landeten, waren sie schon spurlos verschwunden.

Die Portugiesen blieben nicht. Als 1625 die Engländer mit ihrem Schiff *The Olive Blossom* auf dem unter dem heutigen Namen Holetown bekannten Gebiet landeten, fanden sie die Insel unbewohnt vor, und beanspruchten sie für König James von England. 80 Siedler und 10 Sklaven ließen sich am 17. Februar 1627 nieder und trugen dazu bei, Barbados in eine von Englands reichsten Kolonien zu verwandeln.

Seit dem Tag der Unabhängigkeit am 30. November 1966 hat sich Barbados zu einer der meist entwickelten Inseln der Karibik und einem weltweit bewunderten Inselstaat entfaltet. Mit einer Fläche von 430 km2 und einer Einwohnerzahl von mehr als 270.000 befindet sich Barbados laut des HDI (Index der menschlichen Entwicklung) der UN regelmäßig unter den führenden Entwicklungsländern.

Das Land ist in 11 Gemeinden eingeteilt, und Besucher entdecken sehr schnell die atemberaubende Mannigfaltigkeit der Insel. Im Westen und im Süden finden Sie strahlend weiße, von Kokospalmen gesäumte Sandstrände am ruhigen blauen Meer. Im Norden und Osten dagegen treffen dramatische Klippen auf

Bruce Hemming

above & top / participants in the Grand Kadooment

einen stürmischen Ozean. Die sanft geschwungenen Hügel des Scotland District bieten eine willkommene Abwechslung von den Ebenen im Westen und Süden. Die beiden Hauptankunftsorte sind der etwa 18 km von der Hauptstadt Bridgetown entfernte Grantley Adams International Airport sowie der unweit vom Stadtzentrum gelegene Hafen Bridgetown Port.

Was die Unterkünfte auf der Insel angeht, werden hier alle Geschmäcker und Budgets befriedigt: das All-Inclusive-Hotel, das kleine Hotel, das Appartement mit Selbstversorgung, die Pension oder die Villa. Alle stehen unter der Aufsicht des Amtes für Qualitätssicherung des Barbados Tourismusamtes. Hotels und Restaurants bieten Ihnen erlesene Speisen vor einer wunderschönen Kulisse, wobei die Spezialitäten von lokalen Gerichten bis hin zur internationalen Küche reichen – und immer mit dem gewissen karibischen Extra.

Natürlich stehen „Meer, Sand und Sonne" in Barbados auf dem Programm. Doch es gibt noch mehr zu tun: Besichtigungen, Shopping und Sport. Besichtigungen sind wirklich ein Vergnügen – ob vom Helikopter aus mit Blick auf die herrliche Landschaft oder ein Unterwasserabenteuer aus dem U-Boot Atlantis. Außerdem gibt es noch die prächtige Aussicht vom Cherry Tree Hill, den faszinierenden Charme von Sunbury sowie die stolze Ruine Farley Hill.

Die Militärgeschichte von Barbados hat ihre Spuren hinterlassen: das Barbados Museum, ein ehemaliges britisches Militärgefängnis, das heute eine kleine, aber höchst interessante Kuriositätensammlung beherbergt; die Gun Hill Signal Station mit ihrer herrlichen Löwenstatue aus Korallenstein; die Garrison Area, in der sich unter anderem das Bush Hill House befindet – der einzige Ort außerhalb der USA, an dem George Washington übernachtete.

Die Andromeda Botanic Gardens, der Flower Forest und die Orchid World erblühen in exotischer Pracht. Als Zeugnis der Schönheit und Qualität der Blumen in Barbados hat die örtliche Gartenbau-Gesellschaft schon mehr als zehn Goldmedaillen bei der angesehenen Chelsea Flower Show in England gewonnen.

Im Naturschutzgebiet Graeme Hall Swamp können Sie Zugvögel, und bei einem Besuch des Barbados Tierschutzgebietes fast immer Grüne Meerkatzen – das einzige wilde Tier, das in Barbados noch weit verbreitet ist – beobachten. ÷kotouristen können mit Hike Barbados angenehme Ausflüge unternehmen.

Rum wurde erstmals in Barbados destilliert und viele Attraktionen auf der Insel zeugen davon: das Mount Gay Rum Visitors Centre, die Foursquare Rum Factory und Heritage Park sowie das Malibu Visitors Centre. Es ist leicht, sich in der Rumbowle mit ihrem angeblich harmlosen goldenen Schein zu verlieren! Auch die Tour durch die Heimat des lokalen Biers, Banks Breweries, ist überaus beliebt.

Broad Street ist der wichtigste Ort zum Duty-Free-Shopping. Hier gibt es hochwertige Elektrogeräte, Glas- und Kristallornamente, Porzellan, Kameras, Parfüms und alkoholische Getränke. An der West- und Südküste finden Sie Boutiquen mit Designerkleidung sowie erstaunlich vielfältigen Produkten von ansässigen Designern. Das lokale Know-how fließt mit in die Tonwaren, Flecht-

und Papierarbeiten, Malereien sowie Draht- und Muschelarbeiten ein, die es im Pelican Village zu kaufen gibt – hier ist alles garantiert „Made in Barbados".

Eine Sportart ist hier besonders beliebt, und das ist Cricket. Über die Jahre hat die Insel einige der Besten dieses Sports hervorgebracht. Einer davon ist der einzige noch lebende Nationalheld, Sir Garfield Sobers, der weitgehend als „der größte Cricketspieler aller Zeiten" angesehen wird. Doch heutzutage ist auch das Wort „Golf" in aller Munde, sogar Sir Garfields. Golfspieler werden den prächtigen Royal Westmoreland Golf und Country Club sowie den ganzjährig makellosen Golfplatz des Sandy Lane Golf Clubs lieben. Auch der Barbados Golf Club in Durants, Christ Church, ist mit seinem 18-Loch-Platz einen Besuch wert.

Tennis, Pferderennen, Hockey, Jogging, Fußball, Rad fahren, Segelfliegen, Fallschirmsegeln, Surfen, Windsurfen, Wasser- und Jetskifahren, Segeln und Tiefseefischen sind nur einige der weiteren Land- und Wassersportarten, die Sie erleben können. Der letzte Schrei ist das Schwimmen oder besser gesagt Schnorcheln mit Schildkröten, wobei die Saison der Lederschildkröte von März bis Juli und die der Karettschildkröte von April bis Oktober reicht.

Viel Spaß kann man auf dem Jolly Roger Piratenschiff oder dem Harbour Master Flussboot erleben. Ein exklusiveres Erlebnis bieten die kleineren Katamarane, während abends an Land die Insel zum Leben erwacht – bei Shows wie „Bajan Roots and Rhythms" und in Nightclubs wie After Dark, Harbour Lights und The Boatyard.

Besondere Unterhaltung verschaffen während des ganzen Jahres verschiedene Festivals: vom Barbados Jazz Festival im Januar, bei dem eine ausgezeichnete Mischung aus lokalen sowie internationalen Künstlern wie Patti LaBelle, Alicia Keyes und Lionel Richie auftritt, bis hin zur jährlich stattfindenden Holders Season im März, die das Beste aus Oper, Shakespeare und einigen überraschenden Kunstformen präsentiert.

Nach so viel Aufregung muss die Sonne jedoch auch untergehen. Und wenn Sie Glück haben, erhaschen Sie einen Blick auf den seltenen, fast mythischen Grünen Blitz. Doch auch diejenigen, die ihn nicht sehen, werden glücklich sein. Denn sie sind in Barbados und träumen von einem Heim hier. Investition ins Paradies? Gar keine so schlechte Idee!

Bruce Hemming

Barbados: Il fascino dei Caraibi autentici

BARBADOS. Il punto dei Caraibi dove il sole sorge per primo. Barbados. Terra dei pesci volanti dalle scaglie argentate. Barbados. Provate il fascino di un'autentica esperienza caribica. Barbados.

Barbados fu abitata per ben più di 2000 anni dagli indiani Arawak, ai quali fecero seguito i caribi. Benché sull'isola siano stati rinvenuti resti di questi insediamenti indiani, il motivo della loro partenza rimane un mistero. All'arrivo dei portoghesi, nel 1536, gli indiani erano già scomparsi senza traccia.

I portoghesi decisero di non trattenersi e quando approdarono gli inglesi, nel 1625, sulla nave *Olive Blossom* (Fiore d'Ulivo), in una zona oggi nota come Holetown, trovarono un'isola disabitata e la rivendicarono per re Giacomo d'Inghilterra. Il 17 febbraio 1627 seguirono ottanta colonizzatori e 10 schiavi, i quali aiutarono a trasformarla in una delle più ricche colonie inglesi.

Dal 30 novembre 1966, giorno dell'indipendenza, ad oggi, Barbados ha seguito decisamente un percorso volto a renderla una delle isole più sviluppate dei Caraibi e uno dei piccoli stati isolani più ammirati del mondo. Con i suoi 430 chilometri quadrati e 270.000 abitanti, Barbados è anche uno dei paesi in via di sviluppo più avanzati del mondo, secondo l'indice di sviluppo umano delle Nazioni Unite.

Il paese è diviso in 11 parrocchie e il turista si accorgerà ben presto che la diversità del paesaggio lungo il litorale dell'isola è sbalorditiva. A ovest e a sud troviamo palme di cocco che ondeggiano nel vento, schierate lungo spiagge bianche bagnate dalle acque azzurre di un mare tranquillo. A nord e a est, a questa tranquillità si contrappongono ripide scogliere e un oceano turbolento. Le

Bruce Hemming

above & opposite | catamaran cruising off the Saint James coast

above / fish feeding off Saint James

top / jet skiing off the west coast

ondeggianti colline del Scotland District sono una benvenuta distrazione dai terreni pianeggianti dell'ovest e del sud. I due punti di arrivo principali sono l'aeroporto internazionale Grantley Adams, a 17 km dalla capitale, Bridgetown, e il porto di Bridgetown, ad appena 1,6 km dal centro cittadino.

Gli alloggi sull'isola soddisfano tutti i gusti e tutte le tasche, dal tutto compreso ai piccoli alberghi, dagli appartamenti indipendenti, alle pensioni, alle ville, sono tutti soggetti al controllo dell'ufficio di garanzia della qualità dell'ente per il turismo di Barbados. Sia gli alberghi che i ristoranti privati offrono pietanze squisite in ambienti meravigliosi. Che offrano specialità del luogo o internazionali, il sapore è sempre quello unico dei Caraibi,

Barbados garantisce naturalmente il sole, la spiaggia e il mare, ma provvede anche a soddisfare un'altra tripla esigenza: sport, shopping e turismo. Per quanto riguarda il turismo, l'isola offre senza dubbio delle meraviglie, dalle splendide vedute aeree in elicottero alle incredibili avventure subacquee offerte dal sottomarino Atlantis, e poi lo stupendo panorama da Cherry Tree Hill, il fascino incantevole di Sunbury e l'affascinante rovina di Farley Hill.

La storia militare di Barbados ha lasciato le sue tracce: il Barbados Museum, ex-prigione militare britannica, che ospita oggi una piccola ma interessantissima collezione; il Gun Hill Signal Station, antico posto di segnalazione alle navi, con il suo magnifico leone di corallo; la zona di Garrison (guarnigione), ricca di resti storici, come la Bush Hill House, l'unico posto fuori dagli Stati Uniti in cui dormì George Washington.

I giardini botanici di Andromeda, la Flower Forest (foresta dei fiori) e Orchid World (mondo delle orchidee) sono ricchi di fiori esotici. Come testimonianza della bellezza e della qualità dei fiori trovati a Barbados, l'associazione degli orticultori del paese ha vinto più di 10 medaglie d'oro al prestigioso Chelsea Flower Show in Inghilterra.

La Nature Sanctuary (riserva della natura) di Graeme Hall Swamp offre una dimora tranquilla a varie specie di uccelli, principalmente migratori. Visitando la Barbados Wildlife Reserve (riserva degli animali) si è praticamente sicuri di vedere una scimmia verde africana, l'unico animale selvaggio che abbondi sull'isola. L'ecoturista puÚ intraprendere una divertente escursione con Hike Barbados.

Il rum venne distillato per la prima volta a Barbados ed è la ragione d'essere di altre attrazioni: il centro visitatori di Mount Gay Rum; la fabbrica di rum di Foursquare, con il suo parco storico(Heritage Park); il centro visitatori di Malibu. Assuefarsi allo splendore dorato e apparentemente innocuo del "rum punch" non è certo difficile! Non lasciandosi surclassare, anche la sede di produzione della birra locale, Banks Breweries, offre una visita guidata molto frequentata.

Broad Street è la meta principale per gli acquisti duty-free. Qui si possono acquistare prodotti elettronici con marche di prima qualità, soprammobili di vetro e di cristallo, porcellana, macchine fotografiche, profumi e alcolici. Sulla costa occidentale e meridionale troverete anche boutiques di abbigliamento firmato, mentre i numerosi stilisti del luogo realizzano sempre qualcosa di favolosamente diverso. Vedrete questo tocco locale anche nel vasellame, nei dipinti, negli articoli di vimini, carta, fil di ferro, conchiglie, ecc. che troverete al Pelican Village, dove il "Made in Barbados" è garantito.

Il cricket è lo sport venerato più di qualsiasi altro a Barbados. Con il trascorrere degli anni l'isola ha generato alcuni dei migliori giocatori del mondo, il principale dei quali è l'unico eroe vivente del paese: Sir Garfield Sobers – conosciuto in lungo e in largo come il miglior giocatore di cricket di tutti i tempi. Ma oggi anche la parola "golf" è sulla bocca di tutti, anche su quella di Sir Garfield. Gli appassionati di golf s'innamoreranno dello spettacolare Royal Westmoreland Golf and Country Club e del campo perennemente intatto del Sandy Lane Golf Club. Vale la pena anche fare un salto al Barbados Golf Club di Durants a Christ Church, con il suo campo da campionato di 18 buche.

Tennis, equitazione, hockey, footing, calcio, ciclismo, volo librato, parapendio, surfing, windsurfing, sci d'acqua, acquascooter, vela e pesca in alto mare sono solo alcuni degli altri sport terrestri e acquatici che si possono praticare. L'ultima mania è quella di nuotare, o meglio fare lo snorkeling, con le tartarughe marine. La stagione delle tartarughe leatherback è da marzo a luglio, mentre quella delle tartarughe embricate è da aprile a ottobre.

C'è da divertirsi sulla nave pirata Jolly Roger o sulla barca fluviale della capitaneria di porto, nonché sui piccoli catamarani, che offrono un divertimento di tipo più esclusivo. Ritornando a terra, l'isola si riempie di vita la sera con gli spettacoli del dopo cena come "Bajan Roots and Rhythms" e nei locali notturni come After Dark, Harbour Lights e Boatyard.

I festival offrono spettacoli meravigliosi da un capo all'altro dell'anno, dal Barbados Jazz Festival di gennaio, al quale partecipa un'ottima fusione di artisti nazionali e internazionali come Patti LaBelle, Alicia Keyes e Lionel Richie, al più sofisticato Holders Season di marzo, che offre le migliori opere liriche, commedie di Shakespeare e varie forme di espressione artistica del tutto sorprendenti.

Dopo tutto il divertimento, il sole dovrà inevitabilmente tramontare. A questo punto chi è fortunato vedrà il rarissimo e quasi leggendario "lampo verde" di Barbados. Ma anche chi non lo vedrà rimarrà contento, perché si troverà comunque a Barbados, sognando forse di comprarvisi una casa. Un investimento in paradiso? Un'idea niente male!

Barbados:
Viva el auténtico
Caribe

above & opposite / the Cohobblepot concert, part of the annual Crop Over festival

BARBADOS. El lugar del Caribe donde primero sale el sol. Barbados. Hogar del pez plata volador. Barbados. Otra experiencia única en el Caribe. Barbados.

Los indios arahuacos habitaron la isla durante más de 2.000 años y más tarde la poblaron los caribes. A pesar de haberse encontrado indicios de la presencia de estos pueblos en Barbados, los detalles exactos de su partida están rodeados de un aura de misterio. Para cuando los portugueses llegaron en 1536, los indios habían desaparecido sin dejar rastro.

Pero los portugueses tampoco se quedaron. Cuando los ingleses, que vinieron a bordo del *Olive Blossom*, desembarcaron en 1625 en una zona que ahora se llama Holetown, se la encontraron deshabitada y la reclamaron para el rey James de Inglaterra. Tras ellos, el 17 de febrero de 1627, llegaron 80 colonos y diez esclavos que contribuyeron a hacer de ella una de las colonias más ricas de Inglaterra.

Desde el día de su Independencia -el 30 de noviembre de 1966- hasta la actualidad, Barbados ha recorrido una determinada andadura hasta convertirse en una de las islas más desarrolladas del Caribe, así como en uno de los estados compuestos de islas pequeñas más admirados del mundo. Con una superficie de 430 kilómetros cuadrados y una población de más de 270.000 habitantes, Barbados se encuentra constantemente entre los principales países en vías de desarrollo según el Índice de Desarrollo Humano de la ONU.

El territorio está dividido en 11 distritos y cuenta con una sorprendente diversidad en sus zonas periféricas, algo que los visitantes notan enseguida. En el oeste y el sur, las palmeras se mecen a lo largo de playas de blancas arenas ante un tranquilo mar azul. Este escenario contrasta con los acantilados

Bruce Hemming

top & above / performers at the Crop Over Cohobblepot concert

dramáticos y el océano turbulento del norte y el este. Las onduladas colinas de Scotland District también suponen un agradable cambio tras las planicies del oeste y el sur. Los dos puntos de llegada principales son el Aeropuerto Internacional Grantley Adams, a 18 kilómetros de la capital, Bridgetown, y el puerto de Bridgetown, a tan sólo un kilómetro y medio del centro de la ciudad.

La isla dispone de alojamiento para todos los gustos y presupuestos: hoteles de pensión completa, hoteles pequeños, apartamentos independientes, hostales y villas. Todos ellos supervisados por el *Quality Assurance Department of the Barbados Tourism Authority* (Departamento de Control de Calidad de la Oficina de Turismo de Barbados). Dichos establecimientos ofrecen comidas exquisitas en bellos entornos, al igual que los restaurantes privados, que se especializan en platos del lugar o en cocina internacional servida con un sabor caribeño único.

Barbados ofrece el típico trío vacacional "sol + mar + arena", pero también brinda otro trío clásico del turismo: "visitas a lugares de interés + compras + actividades deportivas". Las visitas a lugares de interés son sin duda un verdadero lujo que va desde viajes en helicóptero y espléndidas vistas aéreas, a fabulosas aventuras subacuáticas en el submarino *Atlantis*. También hay que mencionar las esplendidas vistas desde Cherry Tree Hill, el exquisito encanto de Sunbury y las misteriosas ruinas de Farley Hill.

La historia militar de Barbados ha dejado su huella en el Museo de Barbados, una antigua prisión militar británica que contiene hoy una pequeña pero muy interesante colección; la *Gun Hill Signal Station* y su majestuoso león de piedra coralina; y el *Garrison Area*, con abundantes reliquias entre las que se incluye *Bush Hill House*, el único lugar fuera de los Estados Unidos donde durmió George Washington.

Las flores exóticas abundan en los Jardines Botánicos *Andromeda*, en *Flower Forest* y *Orchid World*. Prueba de la belleza y la calidad de las flores que existen en Barbados son las diez Medallas de Oro logradas por su *Horticultural Society* en el prestigioso *Chelsea Flower Show* de Inglaterra.

Otras dos visitas interesantes son el Santuario de la Naturaleza en *Graeme Hall Swamp*, hogar sobre todo de pájaros migratorios, y la Reserva de Flora y Fauna de Barbados, donde es casi seguro el avistamiento del mono verde africano, el único animal salvaje que abunda en la isla. Para el ecoturista también existe una estupenda excursión organizada por *Hike Barbados*.

Aquí fue donde se destiló ron por primera vez y el licor es la excusa perfecta para otras visitas: el Centro de Visitantes Mount Gay Rum; la fábrica de ron *Foursquare* y el *Heritage Park*; el Centro de Visitantes *Malibu*. A pesar del inofensivo aspecto de su brillo dorado, uno se puede volver adicto al ponche de ron... Para no ser menos, *Banks Breweries*, hogar de la cerveza del lugar, proporciona asimismo un tour muy popular.

Broad Street es el principal lugar para las compras libres de impuestos. En sus tiendas se pueden encontrar las mejores marcas de objetos electrónicos, ornamentos de vidrio y cristal, porcelanas, cámaras, perfumes y licores. Las boutiques de la costa oeste y de la costa sur ofrecen ropa de diseño, mientras que los numerosos diseñadores locales garantizan una producción marcadamente diferente. El toque local también se aprecia en la cerámica, la cestería, la papelería, los cuadros, los trabajos en alambre y con conchas... De todo esto hay en *Pelican Village*, donde el *made in Barbados* está garantizado.

En Barbados existe un deporte que se venera por encima de todos los demás: el críquet. A lo largo de los años, de la isla han salido algunos de los mejores jugadores de este deporte, entre los que destaca el único héroe nacional vivo, Sir Garfield Sobers, reconocido como "el mejor jugador de críquet que jamás haya existido en el mundo". No obstante, hoy en día todos hablan de golf, incluso Sir Garfield. A los amantes de este deporte les encantará el glorioso *Royal Westmoreland Golf and Country Club* y los campos siempre impecables del *Sandy Lane Golf Club*. Y no estaría de más que probasen el *Barbados Golf Club* de *Durants* en Christ Church y su campo de campeonato con 18 hoyos.

El tenis, los caballos, el jockey, las carreras, el fútbol, la bicicleta, el ala delta, el parapente, el surfing, el windsurfing, el esquí acuático, las motos de agua, la vela y la pesca en alta mar son sólo algunos de los otros deportes de tierra y mar que es posible practicar. Lo ultimísimo es nadar o, más concretamente, hacer snorkel con las tortugas. La época de la tortuga laúd es entre marzo y julio y la de la tortuga carey, de abril a octubre.

El barco pirata *Jolly Roger* y la embarcación fluvial *Harbour Master* son dos actividades más a disfrutar. Los catamaranes de menor tamaño permiten un tipo de entretenimiento más exclusivo, mientras que en tierra firme la isla se anima por las noches con espectáculos para después de cenar tales como el *Bajan Roots and Rhythms* y los clubes nocturnos como *After Dark, Harbour Lights* y el *Boatyard*.

Los festivales proporcionan otra oferta de ocio especial durante todo el año. Tal es el caso del *Barbados Jazz Festival*, que se celebra en enero y que ya ha presentado una excelente combinación de actuaciones de lugareños con artistas internacionales como Patti LaBelle, Alicia Keyes y Lionel Richie. O el sofisticado *Holders Season*, que acontece en marzo y ofrece lo mejor en opera, Shakespeare y diversas formas artísticas sorprendentes.

Tras la diversión y el ajetreo es inevitable que el sol se ponga. Ese es el momento en que los afortunados verán el extraño y casi mítico destello verde. Y quienes no lo vean, seguirán felices porque aún están en Barbados y sueñan con comprarse una casa en la isla. ¿Invertir en el paraíso? ¡Pues no es tan mala idea!

Hansib Publications is grateful for the support given by the following businesses and organisations

Dialling Codes

Dialling from the Caribbean and North America: 1 246

Dialling from the United Kingdom: 001 246

Accommodation & Real Estate

Alleyne Real Estate (A Division of Jennifer Alleyne Ltd.)
Molyneux House
Sandy Lane
St. James
Tel: 432-1159
Fax: 432-2733
Email: info@jalbarbados.com

Caribbean Lifestyles Ltd
ISL Complex Lots A B & C
Warrens Industrial Park
St. Michael
Tel: 428-3554
Fax: 425-2324
Email: info@caribbean-lifestyles.com

Island Gold Realty & Fairways Real Estate
The Barbados Golf Club
Durants
Christ Church
and at
Rockley Golf & Country Club
Rockley
Christ Church
Tel: 420-8789 / 435-7852/62
Fax: 435-8268
Email: fairways@caribsurf.com

Realtors Ltd
Holetown
St. James BB 24116
Tel: 432-6930
Fax: 432-6919
Email: info@realtorslimited.com

The Lakes Development Co. Ltd
Mount Brevitor
St. Peter
Tel: 422-6639
Fax: 422-6640
Email: lyndad@thelakescaribbean.com

Activities

Atlantis Submarines Barbados Inc.
The Shallow Draught
Bridgetown
Tel: 436-8968 ext 231
Fax: 436-8828
Email: rmyers@atlantissubmarines.com

Earthworks (is no ordinary) Pottery
2 Edghill Heights
Shop Hill
St. Thomas
Tel: 425-0223
Fax: 425-3224
Email: eworks@caribsurf.com

Flower Forest of Barbados Ltd
Richmond
St. Joseph
Tel: 433 8152
Fax: 433-8365
Email: ffl@sunbeach.net

Graeme Hall Nature Sanctuary
Worthing
Christ Church
Tel: 435-9727
Fax: 435-6330
Email: hroberts@caribsurf.com

Ocean Park
Balls Complex
Christ Church
Tel: 420-7405
Fax: 420-7406
Email: info@oceanparkbarbados.com

Reefers & Wreckers
Timothy House
Orange Street
Speightstown
St. Peter
Tel: 422-5450
Fax: 422-5450
Email: scubadiving@caribsurf.com

Sunbury Great House
Sunbury Plantation
St. Philip
Tel: 423-6270
Fax: 423-5863
Web: www.barbadosgreathouse.com

Architects

Gillespie & Steel Associates Ltd
Dormers Prior Park
St. James
Tel: 425-1356
Fax: 424-0334
Email: admin@gillespieandsteel.com / dspink@gillespieandsteel.com

Automotive Care, Retail and Servicing

Automotive Art
P.O. Box 72W
Wildey Industrial Park
St. Michael
Tel: 426-1800
Fax: 436-5743
Email: info@automotiveart.com

Banks

RBC Royal Bank of Canada
P.O. Box 68
Bridgetown
Tel: 467-4126
Fax: 426-4139
Email: susan.blackett@rbc.com

RBTT Bank Barbados Ltd
Lower Broad Street
Bridgetown
St. Michael
Tel: 431-2500
Fax: 429-3556
Email: info@bb.rbtt.com

Scotiabank
Managing Director's Office Caribbean East
1st Floor CGI Tower
Warrens
St. Michael
Tel: 431-3071
Fax: 421-7110
Email: marcelle.greenidge@scotiabank.com

Bookstores

Cloister Bookstore Ltd
Hicks & Cowell Streets
Bridgetown
Tel: 426 2662/228 0033
Fax: 429 7269

Pages Book Stores
Duty Free Caribbean
24 Broad Street
Bridgetown
Tel: 227-1336
Fax: 436-9813

Business / Conglomerate

Ansa McAl (Barbados) Ltd
Wildey
St. Michael BB 14007
Tel: 434-2900
Fax: 228-1519
Email: headoffice@mcalbds.com

Barbados Shipping & Trading Co. Ltd
P.O. Box 1227C
Warrens
St.Michael B11000
Tel: 417-5110
Fax: 417-5116
Email: info@bsandtco.com

Goddard Enterprises Limited
2nd Floor Mutual Building
Lower Broad Street
Bridgetown
St. Michael
Tel: 430-5700
Fax: 436-8934
Email: ashwell_thomas@goddent.com

Construction

Abacus Builders Inc
Prior Park, St. James
Tel: 421-7939
Fax: 421-7488
Email: info@abacus-builders.com

Innotech Services Ltd
ISL Complex Lots A B & C
Warrens
St. Michael
Tel: 425-2065
Fax: 425-2324
Email: info@innotech-services.com

Tower Bucknall Austin
Dover Court
Maxwell Main Road
Christ Church
Tel: 420-3501
Fax: 420-4675
Email: tower@towerbucknall.com

Cultural

National Cultural Foundation Barbados
West Terrace
St. James
Tel: 424-0909
Fax: 424-0916
Email: wayne-webster@thencf.org

Distribution

LASCO (Barbados) Limited
Maxwell
Christ Church
Tel: 429-2328
Fax: 426-1730
Email: creid-sealey@lascobarbados.com

Education

The Codrington School
St. John
Tel: 423-2570
Fax: 423-0095
Email: info@codrington.edu.bb

Financial Investment & Services

Barbados Public Workers' Co-Op Credit Union Ltd
Olive Trotman House
Keith Bourne Complex
Belmont Road
Bridgetown
Tel: 434-2667
Fax: 437-8745
Email: karen.headley-lucas@bpwccul.bb

Consolidated Finance Co. Limited
Tamarind
Upper Collymore Rock
St. Michael
Tel: 467-2350
Fax: 426-8626 / 228-2318
Email: info@consolidated-finance.com

KPMG
Hastings
Christ Church
Tel: 427-5230
Fax: 427-7123
Email: info@kpmg.bb

Golf / Polo Clubs

Barbados Golf Club
Durants
Christ Church
Tel: 428 8463
Fax: 420-8205
Email: cjordan@barbadosgolfclub.com /
mail@barbadosgolfclub.com

Royal Westmoreland
Westmoreland
St. James
Tel: 422-4653
Fax: 422-3021
Email: rwadmin@royal-westmoreland.com

Apes Hill Club
Apes Hill
St. James
Tel: 432-4500
Fax: 432-4501
Email: lwilliams@apeshillclub.com

Government

Barbados Defence Force
St. Ann's Fort
Garrison
St. Michael
Tel: 436 6185
Fax: 429-9678
Email: dowridge.d@bdf.gov.bb

Government (Promotion of International Business)

Barbados International Business Promotion Corporation
The Corporate Center
Bush Hill
Bay Street
St. Michael
Tel: 435-6570
Fax: 429-7996

Health Care Products

Carib Rehab Ltd
Friendship Plantation
Hothersal Turning
St. Michael
Tel: 427-9687
Fax: 436-0704
Email: caribrehab@sunbeach.net

Heritage Attraction

St. Nicholas Abbey
Cherry Tree Hill
St. Peter
Tel: 422-8725
Fax: 432-2976
Email:
heritagetourism@stnicholasabbey.com

Horticulture

Barbados Horticultural Society
Balls Plantation
Christ Church
Tel: 428-5889 / 429-3690
Fax: 428-5889
Email: hortsociety@sunbeach.com

Hotels & Resorts

**Barbados Beach Club
(All Inclusive Resort)**
Maxwell Coast Road
Christ Church
Tel: 428-9900
Fax: 428-8905
Email: holidays@barbadosbeachclub.com

Cobblers Cove Hotel
St. Peter
Tel: 422-2291
Fax: 422-1460
Email: rstevenson@cobblerscver.com

Divi South Winds Hotel & Beach Club
St. Lawrence Main Road
Christ Church
Tel: 428-7181
Fax: 420-2673
Email: guests_southwinds@caribsurf.com

Elegant Hotels Group
Tamarind Cove
Paynes Bay
St. James
Tel: 432-6525
Tel: US 1800-326-6898
Tel: UK 0800-587-3427
Fax: 432-6412
Email: reservations@eleganthotels.com

Intimate Hotels of Barbados
BHTA Building
4th Avenue
Belleville
St. Michael
Tel: 436-2053
Fax: 436-3748
Email:
information@intimatehotelsbarbados.com

**Needham's Point Holdings Ltd
with Hilton as Manager**
Needhams Point
St. Michael
Tel: 467-5656
Fax: 228-7730
Email: marilyn.soper@hilton.com

Ocean One
Maxwell Coast Road
Christ Church
Tel: 418-8086
Fax: 428-0205
Email: choward@chickmontfoods.net

Palm Beach Hotel Group
Amaryllis Beach Resort
Garrison Historic Area
Palm Beach
Hastings
Christ Church
Tel: 438 8000
Fax: 426-9566
Email:
alvin.jemmott@palmbeachhotelgroup.com

Sea Breeze Beach Hotel
Maxwell Coast Road
Christ Church
Tel: 428-2825
Fax: 428-2872
Email: reservations@sea-breeze.com

South Beach Resort
Rockley at Accra Beach
Christ Church
Tel: 435-8561
Fax: 435-8594
Email:
reservations@southbeachbarbados.com

Treasure Beach Hotel
Paynes Bay
St. James
Tel: 432-1346
Fax: 432-1094
Email: hamish@treasurebeachhotel.com

Ice Cream/Public Cold Storage Facility

BICO Ltd
Harbour Industrial Park
Bridgetown BB11145
Tel: 430-2100
Fax: 426-2198
Email: admin@bicoltd.com

Information Technology

IBM World Trade Corporation
Radley Court
Collymore Rock
St. Michael
Tel: 426-0670
Fax: 429-4684
Email: dthomas@bb.ibm.com

Illuminat (Barbados) Ltd
Geddes Grant Building
Whitepark Road
St. Michael
431-5600
Fax: 427-6089
Email:
michael.armstrong@illuminatnm.com

Information Technology/Security

Advanced Business Systems (ABS) Inc
42 Warrens Industrial Park
St. Michael BB 22026
Tel: 417-5600
Fax: 417-5611
Email: sales@abscards.com

Insurance

British American Insurance Co
Cnr. Brittons Cross Road & Collymore
Rock
St. Michael
Tel: 431-4400 ext 4402
Fax: 436-8820
Email: bai@babdos.com.bb

Co-operators General Insurance Co. Ltd
3rd Floor BNB Building
Independence Square
Bridgetown
Tel: 431-8600
Fax: 430-9148
Email: insure@coopgeneral.com

Island Heritage Insurance Co. Ltd
Suite 15 1st Floor
Thomas Daniel Building
Hincks Street
Bridgetown
Tel: 426-2218
Fax: 426-2224
Email: customerservice@islandheritage.bb

Sagicor Life Inc.
Sagicor Corporate Centre
Wildey
St. Michael
Tel: 467-7500
Fax: 426-2922
Email: info@sagicor.com

Manufacturers / Distributors

Arawak Cement Company Limited
Checker Hall
St. Lucy
Tel: 439-9880
Fax: 439-7976
Email: arawak@arawakcement.com.bb

BHL - Banks Holdings Limited
P.O. Box 507C
Wildey
St. Michael BB11000
Tel: 429-2113
Fax: 427-0772
Email: scambridge@banksholdings.com.bb

Rose and Laflamme (Barbados) Ltd
Newton Industrial Park
Christ Church
Tel: 428 8841
Fax: 420-8523
Email: roselaflamme@sunbeach.net

Sunpower (1999) Ltd
Searles Factory
Christ Church
Tel: 428-0634
Fax: 428-0740
Email: hjordan@sunpowR.com

Maps

Skyviews Caribbean Ltd
PO Box 3119
Moletown
St James
Tel: 434 / 3434/5
Fax: 434 / 3435
Email: info@skyviews.com

Photography

Brooks Latouche Photography Ltd
18 Pine Road Opp. 5th Avenue
Belleville
St. Michael
Tel: 427 2313
Fax: 437-3471
Email: rbrooks@brookslatouche.com
Web: www.brookslatouche.com

Restaurants

Bubba's Sports Bar & Restaurant
Rockley Main Road
Worthing
Christ Church BB 15150
Tel: 435 - 6217 / 435-8731
Fax: 435-8732
Email: bubbas2@caribsurf.com

Daphne's Restaurant
Paynes Bay
St. James
Tel: 432-2731
Fax: 432-5161
Web: www.daphnesbarbados.com

Josefs Restaurants
St. Lawrence Gap
Christ Church
Tel: 420-7638
Fax: 420-7639
Email: josefsrestaurant@hotmail.com

Pauls Enterprises Ltd
Rylands
6 5th Avenue
Belleville
St. Michael
Tel: 436-1739
Email: james@paulsltd.com

Pisces Restaurant
St. Lawrence Gap
Christ Church
Tel: 435-6564
Fax: 435-6439
Email: piscesrestaurant@caribsurf.com

The Restaurant at Southsea
St. Lawrence Gap
Christ Church
Tel: 420-7423
Fax: 428-9284
Email: restaurantsouthsea@caribsurf.com

Wow Group Ltd
T/A Lone Star Restaurant & Hotel
Mount Standfast
St. James
Tel: 419-0599
Fax: 419-0597
Email: wowgroupltd@sunbeach.com

Security Services

G4S Security Services (Barbados) Ltd
Brighton Spring Garden
St. Michael
Tel: 417-7233
Fax: 421-7574
Email: security@bb.g4s.com

JE Security Systems & Services Inc
Lot 2B
Edghill
St. Thomas
Tel: 417-0520
Fax: 425-0205
Email: sales@jesecurity.com /
jesecurity@sunbeach.net

Services

Barbados Coalition of Service Industries
14 Pine Plantation Road
St. Michael
Tel: 429 5357
Fax: 429 5352
Email: bcsi@sunbeach.net

Barbados Institute of Management & Productivity
BIMAP Drive
Wildey
St. Michael
Tel: 431-4238
Fax: 429-6733
Email: rudy@bimap.com.bb

Barbados Tourism Investment Inc
Ground Floor
Old Town Hall building
Cheapside
Bridgetown BB11142
Tel: 426-7085
Fax: 426-7086
Email: btii@tourisminvest.com.bb

Bridgetown Cruise Terminals Inc
Deep Water Harbour
Bridgetown Port
Tel: 431-0386
Fax: 431-9032
Email:
rmorris@bridgetowncruiseterminals.com

WAMCO Data Management
Suite 103
Building 4
Harbour Industrial Park
Bridgetown
St. Michael
Tel: 437-3154
Fax: 434-8883
Email: info@wamcodm.com

Shipping

Eric Hassell & Son Ltd
Carlisle House
Hincks Street
Bridgetown
St. Michael
Tel: 436 6102
Fax: 429-3416
Email: erica@erichassell.com

Laparkan B'dos Ltd
Suite 103 Building 8
Harbour Industrial Estate
St. Michael
Tel: 436-5322
Fax: 420-7068
Email: lpkbgisales@caribsurf.com /
jmorrislpk@caribsurf.com

Tropical Shipping
Goddards Complex
Fontabelle
St. Michael
Tel: 426-9990
Fax: 426-7750
Email: barbados@tropical.com

Telecommunications

Cable & Wireless (Barbados) Limited
Wildey
St. Michael
Tel: 292 5050
Fax: 431-0068
Email: emerson.hewitt@cw.com

Trade & Industry

Armstrong Agencies Ltd
Lot 2 Lower Estate
St. Michael
Tel: 426-2767
Fax: 429-2767
Email: andy@armstrong.com.bb

Atlantis Sea Food Inc.
Unit 6A Building 3
Pine Industrial Estate
St. Michael BB 11103
Tel: 429-0594
Fax: 429-0610
Email: atlantissea@sunbeach.net

Barbados Packaging Industries Ltd
Box 3859 Applewhaites
St Thomas
Tel: 425-7225
Fax: 425-2077
Email: customerservice@BPI.com.bb

Chickmont Foods
Balls Plantation
Christ Church
Tel: 418-8086
Fax: 428-0205
Email: choward@chickmontfoods.net

Cole's Printery Ltd
P.O. Box 232
Wildey
St. Michael
Tel: 427-5153
Fax: 427-5445
Email: james@colesprintery.com

Collins Limited
4A Warrens Industrial Park
St. Michael
Tel: 425-4550
Fax: 424-9182
Email: colcar@caribsurf.com

InterAmericana Trading Corporation
P.O. Box 98
Warrens
St. Michael
Tel: 417-8000
Fax: 421-6438
Email: micedw@itcbgi.com

Moore Paragon
Wildey
St. Michael
Tel: 429-6762
Fax: 436-8928
Email: agmoore@caribsurf.com

Mount Gay Distilleries Ltd
Brandons
St. Michael
Tel: 425-9899
Fax: 425-8338
Email: geoffrey.markle@remy-cointreau.com

Ocean Fisheries Ltd
31 Warrens Industrial Park
St. Michael
Tel: 425-3695
Fax: 425-2235
Email: sales@ocean-fisheries.com

Stansfeld Scott & Co. Ltd
P.O. Box 30
Spring Garden Highway
Bridgetown
St. Michael
Tel: 426-4410
Fax: 426-2958
Email: Jayshree@stansfeldscott.com

The Sol Group
2nd Floor Mahogany Court
Wildey
St. Michael
Tel: 431-4800
Fax: 431-4270
Email: info@solpetroleum.com

Williams Industries Inc
Warrens
St. Michael
Tel: 425-2000
Fax: 425-2941
Email: jfrancis@williamsind.com /
jpayne@williamsind.com /
bizzy@williamsind.com

Weddings

Weddings...beyond Your Imagination!!
154 Atlantic Shores
Christ Church
Tel: 420-4832
Fax: 420-4832
Email: cupid@barbadosweddings.com

Barbados Tourism Authority Offices Worldwide

BARBADOS – Headquarters
Barbados Tourism Authority
PO Box 242
Harbour Road
Bridgetown, Barbados WI
Tel: 246 427 2623/246 427 2624
Fax: 426 4080
Email: btainfo@visitbarbados.org

AUSTRALIA
10th Floor
1 Bligh Street
Sydney 2000
Tel: 61 2 8080 5666
Fax: 61 2 9221 9800

CANADA
Barbados Tourism Authority
105 Adelaide Street West
Suite 1010, Toronto
Ontario M5H IP9
Tel: 416 214 9880
Freephone: 1 800 268 9122
Fax: 416 214 9882
Email: canada@visitbarbados.org

FRANCE
Office du Tourisme de la Barbade
c/o Tropic Travel
48 rue des Petites Ecuries
75010 Paris
Tel: +33 1 47 708282
Fax: +33 1 47 708283
Email: barbade@tropic-travel.com

GERMANY
The Mangum Group
Sonnenstrasse 9
D-80331 Munchen
Tel: 49 (0)89 23 66 21 52
Fax: 49 (0)89 23 66 21 99

PUERTO RICO
Barbados Tourism Authority
PMB 160, 405 Esmeralda Avenue
Guaynabo 00969-4457
Tel: (787) 396-6772/(787) 782 2656
Email: gdrosco@aol.com

UNITED KINGDOM
Barbados Tourism Authority
263 Tottenham Court Road
London WIT 7LA
Tel: 020 7636 9448
Fax: 020 7637 1496
Email: btauk@visitbarbados.org

UNITED STATES OF AMERICA
Barbados Tourism Authority
800 Second Avenue
New York, New York 10017
Tel: 212 986 6516/8
Freephone: 800 221 9831
Fax: 212 573 9850
Email: btany@visitbarbados.org

Barbados Tourism Authority
Suite 1207
3440 Wilshire Boulevard
Los Angeles, California 90010
Tel: 213 380 2198
Fax: 213 384 2763
Email: btala@visitbarbados.org

Barbados Tourism Authority
150 Alhambra Circle
Suite 1000, Coral Gables
Florida 33134
Tel: 305 442 7471
Fax: 305 774 9497
Email: btamiami@visitbarbados.org

VENEZUELA
Av. Venezuela Con Calle Mohedano
Hotel JW Marriott Local 4
El Rosal Caracas
Tel: 0212 951 2738/0800 225 26
Fax: 0212 952 8139
Email: jrmccs@cantv.net

Accommodation: Apartments

Adulo Apartments
Rockley
Christ Church
Tel: 426 6811
email: aduloapartments@sunbeach.net

Anthurium Suites
Worthing
Christ Church
Tel: 435 7439
email: asuite@sunbeach.net

Banyan Court Apartments
Chelsea Road
St Michael
Tel: 426 2815

Bonanza Apartments
Tel: 428 8367
email: bonanza@sunbeach.net
www.funbarbados.com

Carib Blue Apartments
Dover Terrace
Christ Church
Tel: 428 2290

Carvette Apartments
Back Ivy
St Michael
Tel: 426 1548

Caspian Beach Apartments
Sand Street
Speightstown
St Peter
Tel: 422 2520

Chateau Blanc Apartments on the Sea
1st Avenue
Worthing
Christ Church
Tel: 435 7518
email: chateaublanc@caribsurf.com

Fairholme Hotel & Apartments
Maxwell
Christ Church
Tel: 428 9425

Four Aces Cottages & Apartments
The Knave
St Lawrence
Tel: 428 9441
email: fouraces@sunbeach.net

Gentle Breeze Apartments
Worthing View
Christ Church
Tel: 435 8952

Glenville Cottages
Brownes Gap
Hastings
Christ Church
Tel: 228 7413
email: cottagesinagarden@caribsurf.net

Golden Sands Apartment Hotel
Maxwell
Christ Church
Tel: 428 8051

Hastings Towers
Caribbee Beach Hotel
Hastings
Christ Church
Tel: 426 3334

Healthy Horizons
Hastings Main Road
Christ Church
Tel: 435 9195

Homar Rentals Ltd
Europa Palm Avenue
Sunset Crest
Tel: 432 6750
www.barbadostraveller.com

Karekath Apartments on the Beach
St Peter
Tel: 425 1498
www.karekathapartments.com

Kirba Apartments
33 Blue Waters
Christ Church
Tel: 427 0868

Legend Garden Condos
Mullins Bay
St Peter
Tel: 422 8369

Magic Isle Beach Apartments
Rockley Beach
Christ Church
Tel: 435 6760
email: magicisle@caribsurf.com

Maresol Beach Apartments
St Lawrence Gap
Christ Church
Tel: 428 9300
email: maresolapt@sunbeach.net
www.maresolbeach.net

Melbourne Apartments
Stanmore Crescent
St Michael
Tel: 425 1153

Melrose Beach Apartments
Worthing
Christ Church
Tel: 435 7985

Merriville Apartments Ltd
Rockley Terrace
Christ Church
Tel: 435 6712

Miami Beach Apartments
Enterprise Drive
Christ Church
Tel: 428 5387
email: miamiapt@caribsurf.com

Montrowe Apartments
Mangrove Street
St Philip
Tel: 435 5433

Nautilus Beach Apartments
Bay Street
St Michael
Tel: 426 3541
email: nautilusbeach@caribsurf.com

Ocean II Hotel Apartments
Dover Gardens
St Lawrence Gap
Christ Church
Tel: 420 3129

Ocean Spray Apartments
Inch Marlow
Christ Church
Tel: 428 5426
www.oceansprayapts.com

Oleander Beach Apartments
Worthing
Christ Church
Tel: 430 9630
email: oleanderbeach@sunbeach.net

Pirates Inn
Hastings
Christ Church
Tel: 426 6273

Point View Apartments
Inch Marlow
Christ Church
Tel: 428 8629

Roman Beach Apartments
Miami Beach
Oistins
Christ Church
Tel: 428 7635
email: francesroman@sunbeach.net

Rostrevor Apartment Hotel
St Lawrence Gap
Christ Church
Tel: 428 9298

Round Rock Apartments-On-Sea
Round Rock
Silver Sands
Christ Church
Tel: 428 7500
email: roundrck@caribsurf.com

Sandy Apartments
Hastings Main Road
Christ Church
Tel: 436 9578

Sea Foam Haciendas
Worthing
Christ Church
Tel: 435 7380

Sierra Beach Apartment Hotel
Hastings
Christ Church
Tel: 429 5620

Skyport Apartments
2 Chancery Lane
Christ Church
email: mertpitt@msn.com

Southern Surf Beach Apartments
Rockley Beach
Christ Church
Tel: 435 6672
www.southernsurfbarbados.com

Standel Apartment Suites
3rd Avenue
Maxwell Coast Road
Christ Church
Tel: 420 5430
email: stanton@caribsurf.com

Summerhayes Apartments
22 Pine Road
St Michael
Tel: 436 5404

Sunflower Apartments
Rockley Terrace
Christ Church
Tel: 429 8941

Sunshine Beach Apartments
Hastings
Christ Church
Tel: 427 1234s

Travellers Palm Apartments
Sunset Crest
St James
Tel: 432 6751

Vida Mejor Villas
Holetown
St James
Tel: 820 3023
email: mejenter@caribsurf.com
www.gotobarbados.com

Walmer Lodge Apartments
St Michael
Tel: 425 1026
email: leroyw@caribsurf.com

White Sands Beach Apartment Hotel
St Lawrence
Christ Church
Tel: 428 7484

Yellow Bird Apartment Hotel
St Lawrence Gap
Christ Church
Tel: 418 8444

Accommodation: Guest Houses

Bay View Guest House
Cnr Baywaters & Brandons
St Michael
Tel: 425 9006
email: bayviewbarbados@hotmail.com

Best E Villas
5 Green Ridge
Prospect
St James
Tel: 425 9751
www.bestvillas.com

Broome's Vacation Home
Mt Joy Avenue
Pine Gardens
St Michael
Tel: 426 4955

Crystal Crest Guest House & Apartments
Pine Road
St Michael
Tel: 426 4626

Crystal Waters Guest House
1st Avenue
Worthing
Christ Church
Tel: 435 7514
email: crystalwaters@sunbeach.net

Dolphin Inn Guest House
Dover
Christ Church
Tel: 420 2330

Dover Woods Guest House
Dover Woods
St Lawrence Gap
Christ Church
Tel: 420 6599

Just Home Guest House
Aquatic Gap
Bay Street
St Michael
Tel: 427 3265

Kingsland Palace
446 Kingsland Terrace
Christ Church
Tel: 420 9008

Pegwell Inn
Welches
Christ Church
Tel: 428 6150

Ragged Point Resort
Merricks
St Philip
Tel: 423 8021

Rio Guest House
St Lawrence Gap
Christ Church
Tel: 428 1546

Superville Guest House
3rd Avenue
Pickwick Gap
St Michael
Tel: 426 2831

Tiffany's Guest House
Murielville River Road
St Michael
Tel: 427 4370

Accommodation: Hotels

Abbeville Hotel
Rockley
Christ Church
Tel: 435 7924

Accra Beach Hotel & Resort
Rockley
Christ Church
Tel: 435 8920

Allamanda Beach Hotel
Hastings
Christ Church
Tel: 438 1000
email: vacation@allamandabeach.com
www.allamandabeach.com

Almond Beach Club
Vauxhall
St James
Tel: 432 7840

Almond Beach Village
St Peter
Tel: 422 4900

Amaryllis Beach Resort
Garrison Historic Area
Palm Beach
Hastings
Christ Church
Tel: 438 8000
email: vacation@amaryllisbeachresort.com
www.amaryllisbeachresort.com

Atlantis Hotel & Restaurant
Bathsheba
St Joseph
Tel: 433 9445
email: atlantis_hotel_Barbados@hotmail.com

Barbados Beach Club
Maxwell Coast Road
Christ Church
Tel: 428 9900
www.barbadosbeachclub.com

Baywatch Resort
St Lawrence Gap
Christ Church
Tel: 435 7502
email: info@baywatchbarbados.com

Blue Horizon Hotel
Rockley Beach
Christ Church
Tel: 435 8916
email: bluehrzn@gemsbarbados.com
www.gemsbarbados.com

Blue Orchids Beach Hotel
Worthing
Christ Church
Tel: 435 8057
email: blueorchids@caribsurf.com
www.blueorchidsbarbados.com

Bougainvillea Beach Resort
Maxwell Coast Road
Christ Church
Tel: 418 0990
Email: res@bougainvillearesort.com
www.bougainvillearesort.com

Butterfly Beach Hotel
Maxwell
Christ Church
Tel: 428 9095

Caribbee Beach Hotel
Hastings
Christ Church
Tel: 436 6232
email: caribbee@caribsurf.com

Casuarina Beach Club
St Lawrence Gap
Christ Church
Tel: 428 3600
email: info@casuarina.com
www.casuarina.com

Cobblers Cove Hotel
St Peter
Tel: 422 2291

Coconut Court Beach Hotel
The Garrison Historic Area
Hastings
Christ Church
Tel: 427 1655
email: ccourt@sunbeach.net
www.coconut-court.com

Colony Club Hotel
Porters
St James
Tel: 422 2335
www.eleganthotels.com

Coral Mist Beach Hotel
Worthing
Christ Church
Tel: 435 7712
email: coralmist@caribsurf.com
www.coralmistbarbados.com

Coral Reef Club
St James
Tel: 422 2372

Coral Sands Beach Resort
Worthing
Christ Church
Tel: 435 6617
email: vacation@coralsandsresort.com

Crystal Cove Hotel
Appleby
St James
Tel: 432 2683
www.eleganthotels.com

Discovery Bay Beach Hotel
St James
Tel: 432 1301

Divi Southwinds Hotel & Beach Club
St Lawrence
Christ Church
Tel: 428 7181

Dover Beach Apartment Hotel
St Lawrence
Christ Church
Tel: 428 8076
email: resdover@caribsurf.com
www.doverbeach.com

Escape At The Gap
St Lawrence
Christ Church
Tel: 428 6131

Escape Hotel and Spa
Prospect Bay
St James
Tel: 424 7571

Fairholme Hotel & Apartments
Maxwell
Christ Church
Tel: 428 9425

Gaskins Vacation Inn
The Boulevard Enterprise
Christ Church
Tel: 428 4748

Golden Sands Apartment Hotel
Maxwell
Christ Church
Tel: 428 8051
www.goldensandshotel.com

Grand Barbados Beach Resort
Aquatic Gap
St Michael
Tel: 426 4000

Hilton Barbados
Needhams Point
St Michael
Tel: 426 0200
www.hiltoncaribbean.com/barbados

Intimate Hotels of Barbados
Tel: 436 2053
email:
information@intimatehotelsbarbados.com
www.intimatehotelsbarbados.com

Island Inn Hotel
Aquatic Gap
Garrison
St Michael
Tel: 436 6393

Kings Beach Hotel
Road View
St Peter
Tel: 422 1690
email: kingsbeachhotel@caribsurf.com

Little Arches Hotel
Enterprise Beach
Christ Church
Tel: 420 4689
www.littlearches.com

Little Bay Hotel
St Lawrence Gap
Christ Church
Tel: 435 7246
email: lbay@sunbeach.net

Little Good Harbour
Fort Rupert
Shermans Street
St Peter
Tel: 439 3000
www.littlegoodharbourbarbados.com

Long Beach Club Hotel
Chancery Lane
Christ Church
Tel: 428 6890

Mango Bay Hotel & Beach Club
Second Street
Holetown
St James
Tel: 432 1384
email: mangobay@caribsurf.com
www.mangobaybarbados.com

Melbourne Inn
St Lawrence Gap
Christ Church
Tel: 420 5475

Meridian Inn
Dover
Christ Church
Tel: 428 4051
www.meridianinn.com

Monteray Apartment Hotel
St Lawrence Gap
Christ Church
Tel: 428 9152

Palm Garden Hotel
Worthing
Christ Church
Tel: 435 6406
email: ethel@sunbeach.net

Pirate's Inn
Hastings
Christ Church
Tel: 426 6273
www.pirates-inn.com

Pommarine Hotel
Hastings
Christ Church
Tel: 228 0900
email: pommarine@sunbeach.net

Rainbow Reef Beach Hotel
Dover
Christ Church
Tel: 428 5110
www.rainbowreef.com

Regency Cove Hotels
Hastings
Christ Church
Tel: 435 8924

Rostrevor Apartment Hotel
St Lawrence Gap
Christ Church
Tel: 428 9298
email: rostrevor@caribsurf.com
www.rostrevorbarbados.com

Sandridge Beach Hotel
St Peter
Tel: 422 2361
email: res@sandridgehotel.com
www.sandridgehotel.com

Sandy Bay Beach Club
Worthing
Christ Church
Tel: 435 8000
email: vacation@sandybaybeachclub.com
www.sandybaybeachclub.com

Sandy Lane
St James
Tel: 444 2000
www.sandylane.com

Santosha Retreat & Spa
East Coast Road
St Andrew
Tel: 422 6500

Sea Breeze Beach Hotel
Maxwell Coast Road
Christ Church
Tel: 428 2825

Settlers Beach Villa Hotel
Tel: 422 3052
email: settlers@caribsurf.com
www.settlersbeachhotel.com

Silver Rock Hotel
Silver Sands Beach
Christ Church
Tel: 428 2866
www.gemsbarbados.com

Silver Sands Resort
Christ Church
Tel: 428 6001
email: info@silversandsbarbados.com
www.silversandsbarbados.com

Smugglers Cove Hotel
Paynes Bay
St James
Tel: 432 1741
www.smugglerscovehotel@barbados.org

South Beach Resort & Vacation Club
Rockley at Accra
Christ Church
Tel: 435 8561
email: info@southbeachbarbados.com
www.southbeachbarbados.com

Southern Palms Beach Club
St Lawrence Gap
Christ Church
Tel: 428 7171
www.southernpalms.net

South Gap Hotel
St Lawrence Gap
Christ Church
Tel: 420 7591
www.baywatchbarbados.com

St James Apartment Hotel
Paynes Bay
St James
Tel: 432 0489

Sunset Crest Resort
St James
Tel: 432 6750
www.barbadostraveller.com

Sunswept Hotel
Sunset Complex
Holetown
St James
Tel: 432 2715
email: sunswept@caribsurf.com

Tamarind Cove Hotel
Paynes Bay
St James
Tel: 432 1332
www.eleganthotels.com

The Crane Resort & Residences
St Philip
Tel: 423 6220
www.thecrane.com

The Fairmont Glitter Bay
Porters Bay
St James
Tel: 422 5555

The Fairmont Royal Pavilion
Porters
St James
Tel: 422 5555

The New Edgewater Hotel
Bathsheba
St Joseph
Tel: 433 9900
www.newedgewater.com

The Sandpiper
St James
Tel: 422 2251

The Savanna Hotel
Hastings
Christ Church
Tel: 228 3800
www.gemsbarbados.com

Time Out At The Gap
St Lawrence
Christ Church
Tel: 420 5021
www.gemsbarbados.com

Treasure Beach Hotel
Paynes Bay
St James
Tel: 432 1346
www.treasurebeachhotel.com

Tropical Escape Hotel
Paynes Bay
St James
Tel: 432 5155

Turtle Beach Resort
Dover
Christ Church
Tel: 428 7131
www.eleganthotels.com

Windsurf Beach Hotel
Maxwell
Christ Church
Tel: 420 5862

Worthing Court Hotel
Worthing
Christ Church
Tel: 435 7910

Yellow Bird Apartment Hotel
St Lawrence Gap
Christ Church
Tel: 418 8444
www.yellowbirdhotel.com

Banks

Barbados National Bank Inc
Broad Street
Bridgetown
Tel: 431 5999
www.bnbarbados.com

Barbados Public Workers
Co-operative Credit Union Ltd
Broad Street
Bridgetown
Tel: 434 2667

**Bayshore Bank & Trust
Barbados Corp**
Lauriston House
Lower C'more Rk
St Michael
Tel: 430 8650
www.bayshorebank.com

BOC Global Bank Ltd
Sagicor Corporate Centre
Wildey
St Michael
Tel: 436 1300

Butterfield Bank
Lower Broad Street
Bridgetown
Tel: 431 4500

**Caribbean Financial Services
Corporation**
Radley Court
St Michael
Tel: 431 6400
email: cfsc@sunbeach.net

CIBC Offshore Banking Services Corp
3rd Floor
Warrens
St Michael
Tel: 367 2400

Citicorp Merchant Bank Ltd
ITC Building
Warrens Commercial Centre
St Michael
Tel: 421 7887

Concorde Bank Ltd
Ernst & Young Centre
Bush Hill
St Michael
Tel: 430 5320

Corporate Banking Centre
Tel: 467 8700

DGM Bank & Trust Inc
Chancery House
High Street
Bridgetown
Tel: 427 6364

**Excelsior International Bank & Trust
Corporation**
Tom Adams Financial Centre
Tel: 435 3155

**First Caribbean International Bank
(Barbados) Ltd**
P O Box 503
Warrens
St Michael
Tel: 367 2300
www.firstcaribbeanbank.com

**First Caribbean International Bank
(Offshore) Ltd**
P O Box 180
Rendezvous
Christ Church
Tel: 367 2300

Glenhuron Bank Ltd
Suite 201
1st Floor Building 4
Harbour Business Park
St Michael
Tel: 431 0791

Mancal Bank (Barbados) Inc
3rd Floor
ITC Building
Warrens
St Michael
Tel: 421 8600

Pan Atlantic Bank & Trust Ltd
3rd Floor Musson Building
Hincks Street
St Michael
Tel: 436 9756

Premier Banking Centre
Tel: 367 2300

Royal Bank of Canada
Broad Street
Bridgetown
Tel: 467 4000
www.rbcroyalbank.com/caribbean

RBTT Bank Barbados Ltd
Broad Street
Bridgetown
Tel: 431 2500
www.rbtt.com

The Bank of Nova Scotia
Broad Street
Bridgetown
Tel: 426 7000

Trust & Merchant
Broad Street
Bridgetown
Tel: 367 2300

**The Victoria Bank (Barbados)
Incorporated**
4th Floor Weymouth Corporate Centre
Roebuck Street
St Michael
Tel: 436 5423

Restaurants & Bars

Al Fresco at Treasure Beach
Paynes Bay
St James
Tel: 432 1346

Angry Annies
1st Street
Holetown
St James
Tel: 432 2119

**Bagatelle Great House
Restaurant & Wine Bar**
Bagatelle
St Thomas
Tel: 421 6767

Bajan Blue
Sandy Lane
St James
Tel: 444 2030
www.sandylane.com

Barbecue Barn
Rockley & Warrens
Tel: 436 5000
www.barbecuebarn.com

Bay Bistro Restaurant Wine & Cocktail Bar
Yellow Bird Apartment Hotel
St Lawrence Gap
Christ Church
Tel: 418 9772
email: baybistro@hotmail.com

Bellini's Trattoria
Little Bay Hotel
St Lawrence Gap
Christ Church
Tel: 420 7587
email: little_bay@caribsurf.com

Benny's Bistro & Bar
1st Street
Holetown
St James
Tel: 432 8806

Berts
Rockley
Christ Church
Tel: 435 7924
Pizza Hotline: 431 1111
www.bertsbarbados.com

Bistro Monet
Hastings
Christ Church
Tel: 435 9389
email: bistromonet@hotmail.com

Bistro Too
Settlers Beach
St James
Tel: 422 3245

Blue Rare
1st Street
Holetown
St James
Tel: 432 6557

Brown Sugar
Tel: 426 7684

Bubba's Sports Bar
Rockley
Christ Church
Tel: 435 6217/8731

Café Indigo
Holetown
St James
Tel: 432 0968

Café Sol
St Lawrence Gap
Christ Church
Tel: 420 7655

Café Taboras
The Fairmont Royal Pavilion Hotel
Porters
St James
Tel: 422 5555

Calabaza
Prospect
St James
Tel: 424 4557
email: calabaza@caribsurf.com

Careenage Bar & Grille
Hilton Barbados
Needham's Point
St Michael
Tel: 426 0200 x 5971

Champers
Hastings
Christ Church
Tel: 435 6644
email: champers@caribsurf.com

Champers
Torrington
Skeets's Hill
Rockley
Christ Church
email: champers@caribsurf.com

Coral Reef Club
St James
Tel: 422 2372
Email: coral@caribsurf.com
www.coralreefbarbados.com

Daphne's
Paynes Bay
St James
Tel: 432 2731
www.daphnesbarbados.com

David's Place
Worthing
Christ Church
Tel: 435 9755
email: dinedavids@caribsurf.com
www.davidsplacebarbados.com

Fisherpond Great House
St Thomas
Tel: 433 1754
email: rainchandler@hotmail.com

Flying Fish Restaurant & Bar
South Gap Ocean Hotel
St Lawrence Gap
Christ Church
Tel: 420 7591
email: baybistro@hotmail.com

Groots Bar & Restaurant
Trents
St James
Tel: 432 7435

Harlequin
St Lawrence Gap
Christ Church
Tel: 420 7677
email: harlequin@sunbeach.net

Hotel Atlantis
Bathsheba
St Joseph
Tel: 433 9445
email:
atlantis_hotel_barbados@hotmail.com
www.atlantis.barbados.com

Il Tempio
Fitts Village
St James
Tel: 417 0057

Josef's Restaurant
St Lawrence Gap
Christ Church
Tel: 420 7638
email: josefsrestaurant@hotmail.com
www.diningwithus.net

Kampai @ Josef's Restaurant
St Lawrence Gap
Christ Church
Tel: 420 7638
Email: josefsrestaurant@hotmail.com
www.josefsinbarbados.com

L'Acajou
Sandy Lane
St James
Tel: 444 2030
email:
restaurantreservations@sandylane.com
www.sandylane.com

L'Azure
The Crane Resort
St Philip
Tel: 423 6220
email: info@thecrane.com
www.thecrane.com

La Mer
Port St Charles
St Peter
Tel: 419 2000

Lobster Alive
Wesley House
Bay Street
Bridgetown
Tel: 435 0305
email: lobsteralive@sunbeach.com

Lone Star Restaurant
Mt Standfast
St James
Tel: 419 0599
email: wowgroupltd@sunbeach.net
www.thelonestar.com

Lord Willoughby's Tavern
Bagatelle
St Thomas
Tel: 421 2121

Lonestar
Mount Standfast
St James
Tel: 419 0599
email: wowgroupltd@sunbeach.net
www.thelonestar.com

Lord Willoughby's Tavern
Bagatelle
St Thomas
Tel: 421 2121

Lucky Horshoe Steakhouse Saloon & Slots
Worthing
Christ Church
Tel: 435 5825
www.luckyh.com

Luigis Italian Restaurant
Dover Woods
Dover
Christ Church
Tel: 428 9218
email: simagi@caribsurf.com

Mango's By The Sea
Speightstown
St Peter
Tel: 422 0704
email: mangos@sunbeach.net
www.mangosbythesea.com

Mannie's Suga Suga
Mullins Beach
St Peter
Tel: 419 4511
email: info@mulllinsbeach.com
www.mullinsbeach.com

McBride's Pub & Cookhouse
St Lawrence Gap
Christ Church
Tel: 420 7646

Mosaic Restaurant
South Beach Resort & Vacation Club
Christ Church
Tel: 435 7268

Muscovado Bar & Restaurant
Pommarine Hotel
Marine Gardens
Hastings
Christ Church
Tel: 228 0900
email: pommarine@sunbeach.com
www.pommarinebarbados.com

Naniki Restaurant
Suriname
St Joseph
Tel: 433 1300
email: naniki@lushlife.bb
www.lushlife.bb

Oceans Restaurant
St Lawrence Gap
Christ Church
Tel: 420 7615
email: reservations@oceansbarbados.com
www.oceansbarbados.com

Olives Bar & Bistro
2nd Street
Holetown
St James
Tel: 432 2112
email: olives@caribsurf.com

Opa! Greek Restaurant & Bar
Hastings
Christ Church
Tel: 435 1234
email: greek@opa.bb

Palm Terrace
The Fairmont
Royal Pavilion
St James
Tel: 422 5555
www.fairmont.com

Patisserie & Bistro Flindt
Holetown
St James
Tel: 432 2626
www.flindtbarbados.com

Pisces Restaurant
St Lawrence Gap
Christ Church
Tel: 435 6564
email: piscesrestaurant@caribsurf.com

Players Sports Bar
Worthing
Christ Church
Tel: 426 3596

Ragamuffins
1st Street
Holetown
St James
Tel: 432 1295
email: raga@caribsurf.com

Red Restaurant Brasserie
Hastings Main Road
Christ Church
Tel: 426 4340

Round House Inn Restaurant & Bar
Bathsheba
St Joseph
Tel: 433 9678
email: roundhouse@sunbeach.com
www.roundhousebarbados.com

Sandy Lane
St James
Tel: 444 2030
www.sandylane.com

Sassafras
Derricks
St James
Tel: 432c 6386
email: sassafras@sunbeach.net

Southern Palms Beach Club
St Lawrence Gap
Christ Church
Tel: 428 7171
email: info@southernpalms.net
www.southernpalms.net

Sunbury
St Philip
Tel: 423 6270

Steak House Grill
St Lawrence Gap
Christ Church
Tel: 428 7152
email: info@steakhousebarbados.com
www.steakhousebarbados.com

Sweet Potatoes
St Lawrence Gap
Christ Church
Tel: 420 7668
email: sweetpotatoes@sunbeach.net

The Careenage Bar
Hilton Barbados
Needham's Point
St Michael
Tel: 426 0200 x 5947

The Cliff Restaurant
Tel: 432 1922
email: reservations@thecliffbarbados.com
www.thecliffbarbados.com

The Fish Pot
Little Good Harbour
Shermans
St Peter
Tel: 439 2020
email: littlegoodharbour@sunbeach.net
www.littlegoodharbourbarbados.com

The Garden Terrace
Southern Palms Beach Club
St Lawrence
Christ Church
Tel: 428 7171
email: southernpalms@sunbeach.net
www.southernpalms.net

The Grille at Hilton
Hilton Barbados
Needham's Point
St Michael
Tel: 426 0200
email: info.barbados@hilton.com
www.hiltoncaribbean.com/barbados

The Lighthouse Terrace
Hilton Barbados
Needham's Point
St Michael
Tel: 434 5949
email: info.barbados@hilton.com
www.hiltoncaribbean.com/barbados

The Mews
2nd Street
Holetown
St James
Tel: 4321122

The Plantation
St Lawrence Main Road
Christ Church
Tel: 428 5048
email: plantationrest@sunbeach.net
www.theplantation.bb

The Restaurant at Southsea
St Lawrence Gap
Christ Church
Tel: 420 7423
email: restaurantsouthsea@caribsurf.com
www.therestaurantatsouthsea.com

The Sandpiper
St James
Tel: 432 0968 / 422 2251
email: info@sandpiperbarbados.com
www.sandpiperbarbados.com

The Ship Inn
St Lawrence Gap
Christ Church
Tel: 420 7447
email: info@shipinnbarbados.com
www.shipinnbarbados.com

The Terrace Restaurant
Cobblers Cove Hotel
St Peter
Tel: 422 2291
www.cobblerscove.com

The Tides Restaurant
Balmore Houswe
Holetown
St James
Tel: 432 8356
email: thetidesrest@sunbeach.net
www.tidesbarbados.com

Waterfront Café
The Careenage
Bridgetown
Tel: 427 0093
www.waterfrontcafe.com.bb

Weisers Beach Bar & Restaurant
Brandon Beach
Spring Garden Highway
St Michael
Tel; 425 6450
www.weisersbeachbar.com

Wytukai
Accra Beach Hotel & Resort
Rockley
Christ Church
Tel: 435 8920
Email: reservations@accrabeachhotel.com
www.accrabeachhotel.com

Zafran
Worthing Main Road
Christ Church
Tel: 435 8995
Email: zafran_dining@hotmail.com
www.barbados.org/rest/zafran

Zen
The Crane Resort
St Philip
Tel: 423 6220
email: info@thecrane.com
www.thecrane.com

39 Steps Bistro & Wine Bar
Chattel Plaza
Hastings
Christ Church
Tel: 427 0715

Taxi and Car Hire

Corbins Car Rental
Tel: 427 9531
email: rentals@corbinscars.com

Courtesy Rent-A-Car
Tel: 431 4160
email: reservations@courtesyrentacar.com
www.courtesyrentacar.com

National Car Rentals
Tel: 422 0603
email: sports@carhire.tv
www.carhire.tv

Southern Rentals
Fairholme Gardens
Maxwell
Christ Church
Tel: 428 7013
email: southern@sunbeach.net
www.southernrentalsbarbados.com

Top Car Rentals
Rockley New Road
Christ Church
Tel: 435 0378
www.barbadoscarrentals.com

Tourist Attractions

Beer & Rum Tours

Banks Brewery Tours
Wildey
St Michael
Tel: 228 6486

Mount Gay Rum Tour & Gift Shop
Tel: 425 8757
www.mountgayrum.com

Crafts & Pottery

Best of Barbados Gift Shops
Mall 34
Broad Street
Bridgetown
www.best-of-barbados.com

Chalky Mount Potteries
St Andrew

Earthworks – No Ordinary Pottery
Edgehill Heights 2
St Thomas
Tel: 425 0223
email: eworks@caribsurf.com
www.earthworks-pottery.com

Pelican Craft Centre
Princess Alice Highway
Bridgetown
Tel: 426 0765
email: pelican@bidc.org

Cruises & Game Fishing

Atlantis Adventures
Tel: 436 8929
www.atlantisadventures,com

Big Game Fishing
Tel: 429 1050 or 238 9638
email: sunshine@sunbeach.net

Chantours
Plaza 2
Sunset Crest
St James
Tel: 432 5591
email: chan@caribsurf.com

Cool Runnings Catamaran Cruises
Tel: 436 0911
Email: coolrunningscruises@caribsurf.com
www.coolrunningsbarbados.com

El Tigre Catamaran Sailing Cruises
Tel: 417 7245
email: eltigre@sunbeach.net

Fishing Charters Barbados Inc
Tel: 429 2326; 234 1688
email: burkes@caribsurf.com
www.bluemarlinbarbados.com

Honey Bea 111 Sports Fishing & Cruising
Tel: 428 5344
Email: honeybea111@hotmail.com

MV Harbour Master Day Cruises
Tel: 430 0900
email: tallships@sunbeach.net

Silver Moon Luxury Catamaran Sailing Cruises
Tel: 438 2088
email: oceanadventure@sunbeach.net
www.oceanadventures.bb

Small Cats Catamaran Sailing Cruises
Tel: 231 1585
email: smallcats@sunbeach.net

Thriller Ocean Tours
Tel: 231 8300
email: thriller-oceantours@caribsurg.com

Tiami Luxury Catamaran Cruises
Tel: 430 0900
heritage@tallshipscruises.com

Wet & Wild Tours!
Tel: 429 5337
email: infor@seafari.bb
www.seafari.bb

Equestrian Events

Horse Racing at the Garrison Savannah
email: barturf@sunbeach.net
www.barbadosturfclub.com

Barbados Turf Club
Garrison Savannah
St Michael
email: darmstrong@barbadosturfclub.com

Kendal Racing Stables
Kendal Plantation
St John
Tel: 262 3288

Waterhall Polo Centre
Waterhall Polo Stables
Tel: 262 3282
email: jdrdickson@aol.com

Fitness Clubs

Surfside Wellness Centre
Unit 1B, 5 Wildey Industrial Estate
St Michael
Tel: 436 1024
email: admin@sufsidewellness.com

West One Fitness Studio
DaCostas West Mall
Sunset Crest
St James
Tel: 432 5760
email: yeadon@caribsurf.com

Galleries

Barbados Arts Council
Pelican Craft Centre
Bridgetown
Tel: 426 4385

Beyond Aesthetics Gallery
34 Regency Park
Christ Church
Tel: 228 0485

Freedom Fine Art Gallery
Shop 10
Chattel Village
Holetown
St James
Tel: 432 7047

Gallery of Caribbean Art
Northern Business Centre
Speightstown
St Peter
Tel: 419 0858

Gallery of Caribbean Art
Hilton Hotel
Needham's Point
St Michael
Tel: 434 5765

Gallery of Caribbean Art
Speightstown
St Peter
Tel: 419 0858

Mango's Fine Art Gallery
Queen's Street
Speightstown
St Peter
Tel: 422 0704

On the Wall Gallery
The Tides Restaurant
Holetown
St James
Tel: 432 8356

Queen's Park Gallery
Queen's Park
Constitution Road
Bridgetown
Tel: 427 2345

The Gallery St James
Corner of 2nd Street
Holetown
St James
Tel: 432 2789

The Shell Gallery
Contentment
Gibbes
St Peter
Tel: 422 2593
email: contentment@sunbeach.net

Zemicon Gallery
James Fort Building
Hincks Street
Bridgetown
Tel: 430 0054

Golf

Barbados Golf Club
Durants
Christ Church
Tel: 428 8463
email: teetime@barbadosgolfclub.com
www.barbadosgolfclub.com

Rockley Golf and Country Club
Rockley
Tel: 435 7873

Royal Westmoreland
St James
Tel: 422 4653
www.royal-westmoreland.com

Sandy Lane Golf Club
Sandy Lane
St James
Tel: 444 2500
email: golf@sandylane.com

Helicopter & Parasailing

Helicopter Tours
Bajan Helicopters
Tel: 431 0069
email: helicopters@sunbeach.net
www.bajanhelicopters.com

Parasailing with the Falcon
Tel: 419 0579, 230 4507/9549
email: lourdes@caribnet.net
www.parasailingwiththefalcon.com

Heritage Tours & Museums

Barbados Military Cemetery
Christ Church
Tel: 426 0982

Barbados Museum & Historical Society
Christ Church
Tel: 427 0201
email: museum@caribsurf.com
www.barbmuse.org.bb

Codrington College
St John
email: codrington@sunbeach.net
www.codrington.org

Drax Hall Plantation
St George

East Point Lighthouse
Ragged Point
St Philip

Gun Hill Signal Station
St George

Heritage Park & Rum Factory
St Philip

Historic Plantation House Tours
Sunbury Plantation House
St Philip
Tel: 423 6270
email: sunbury@caribsurf.com

Morgan Lewis Mill
St Andrew

Sam Lord's Castle
St Philip

St John's Church
Nr Hackleton's Cliff
St John

St Nicholas Abbey
St Peter

Sunbury Plantation House
St Philip
Tel: 423 6270
email: sunbury@caribsurf.com

The Garrison Historic Tour
tours@heritagetoursbarbados.com

Tyrol Cot House and Heritage Village
Codrington Hill
St Michael
Tel: 424 2074

Nature & Wildlife

Andromeda Gardens
St Joseph

Animal Flower Caves
North Point
St Lucy
Tel: 439 8797

Barbados Wildlife Reserve
St Peter
Tel: 422 8826

Farley Hill National Park
St Philip

Graeme Hall Nature Sanctuary
Tel: 435 9727
www.graemehall.com

Harrison's Cave
Welchman Hall
St Thomas
Tel: 438 6640
email:
marketingmanager@harrisonscave.com

Marine Park & Visitors Center
Folkestone
Holetown St James
Tel: 422 2314/ 2871

Ocean Park
Balls Complex
Christ Church
Tel: 420 7405
email: info@oceanparkbarbados.com
www.oceanparkbarbados.com

Orchid World
Highway 3B
St George
Tel: 433 0306
email: ffl@sunbeach.net
www.barbados.org/sightseeing/orchidworld

Springvale Eco-Heritage Museum
Welchman Hall
St Thomas

The Flower Forest
Tel: 433 8152
email: ffl@sunbeach.net

Welchman Hall Gully
Welchman Hall
St Thomas
Tel: 438 6671

Nightclubs

Bajan Roots and Rhythms
St Lawrence Main Road
Christ Church
Tel: 428 5048
www.theplantation.bb

Harbour Lights Nightclub
Marine Villa
Bay Street
St Michael
Tel: 436 7225
email: harbourlights@sunbeach.net
www.harbourlightsbarbados.com

Road Tours

Adventure Land 4 x 4 tours
Tel: 418 3687

Island Safari
Tel: 429 5337
email: info@islandsafari.com
www.islandsafari.bb

Johnson's Tours
Tel: 426 5181
email: info@johnsonstours.com
www.johnsonstours.com

Mini-Buggy Safari
Tel: 418 3687s

Shooting

Kendal Sporting (Shooting)
Carrington
St Philip
Tel: 437 5306
email: kendalsports@sunbeach.net
www.kendalsportingclaysbarbados.com

Theatre

The Plantation Theatre
St Lawrence Main Road
Christ Church
Tel: 428 5048
email: plantationrest@sunbeach.net
www.theplantation.bb

Visitor Centre

Malibu Beach Club & Visitor Centre
Brighton
Black Rock
St Michael
Tel: 425 9393

Water sports

Barbados Blue Water Sports at the Hilton
Tel: 434 5764
email: barbadosblue@caribsurf.com
www.divebarbadosblue.com

Hightide Watersports
Coral Reef Club
St James
Tel: 432 0931
email: hightide@sunbeach.net
www.divehightide.com

Reefers & Wreckers Dive Shop
Speightstown
St Peter
Tel: 262 6677
email: scubadiving@caribsurf.com
www.scubadiving.bb

Surf Barbados
Tel: 256 3906
www.surferbarbados.com

Surfing Barbados School & Rentals
Tel: 228 5117
email: burkes@caribsurf.com
www.surfbarbados.com

The Turtle & Shipwreck Snorkel Adventure
Tel: 418 3687

West Side Scuba Centre
Tel: 432 2558
email: peterg@sunbeach.net
www.westsidescuba.com

Publishers

Advocate Publishers (2000) Inc
Fontabelle
St Michael
Tel: 467 2000
email: advocate@sunbeach.net
www.barbadosadvocate.com

Cariglobe Publishing
P O Box 1029
Bridgetown
Tel: 426 8434

Caribbean Publishing Company Ltd
Tel: 946 5361
email: bill@marathondesign.com
www.caribbeanyellowpages.com

Corsons Publications Inc
P O Box 393G
St George
Tel: 437 1122

E-Communications Inc
Suite 101 Building 8
Harbour Industrial Park
St Michael
Tel: 228 2356
email: ecommunications@caribsurf.com

East Caribbean Publications Inc
P O Box 1137
Bridgetown
Tel: 418 0639

Fun 'N' Sun Publishing Inc
205 Rendezvous Gardens
Christ Church
Tel: 435 9608

Hilltop Publications Ltd
11 Cottage Ridge
St George
Tel: 228 9122

Hoyos Publishing Inc
Boarded Hall House
St George
Tel: 437 4592

Insight Publishing Inc
P O Box 761
Bridgetown
Tel: 423 1514

Island Life Magazine
Rendezvous Main Road
Christ Church
Tel: 228 1194
email: sales@islandlife.net
www.islandlife.net

Motoring News
Basix Complex
Oistins
Christ Church
Tel: 420 7947

Nation Graphics
Nation House
P O Box 1203
F'belle
St Michael
Tel: 430 5400
www.nationsnews.com

Sassman Caribbean Publishing Co Ltd
9 Pavillion Court
Hastings
Christ Church
Tel: 430 9075

Select Barbados
P O Box 4135
St Peter
Tel: 419 1616
email: info@selectmags.com

Skyviews Inc
Christ Church
Tel: 434 3434

Complementary Therapies

Barbados Association of Professional Massage Therapies
Tel: 421 7815
email: bdosmassage@hotmail.com

Barbados Association of Reflexologists
Tel: 228 5392

Barbados Reiki Association
Tel: 420 6382
email: barbadosreikiassociation@yahoo.com

Massage & Reflexology
Professional Courses and Treatments
Peacehaven Holistic Therapy School
Tel: 416 3001 or 421 7815
email: peacehaven_school@hotmail.com

Reiki School of Natural Healing
Courses and Treatments, Personal
Development & Feng Shui
Tel: 420 6382
email: reikimaster@yahoo.com

overleaf / sunset – the perfect ending
Weddings...beyond Your Imagination!!